L.I.F.E.

REFLECTIONS

**By
John Michael Palermo**

eBook ISBN: 978-1-965431-45-0
Paperback ISBN: 978-1-965431-46-7
Hardback ISBN: 978-1-965431-47-4

Table of Contents

DEDICATION

To my dearest family & friends... You know who you are. "Y'all" have given me so much hope, inspiration, dedication, commitment, & joy in writing this book. I thank God & anyone out there who knows me as "White Chocolate." This one is for you. "Cheers & Journey Well," my good, great, & captivating souls out there. God bless, & may your universe be blessed, manifested, & lived joyfully.

A LITTLE ABOUT THE AUTHOR

Here is a little background on why I wrote this book. When someone gets bullied emotionally or mentally, they either fall and never get back on their feet, or they rise to the occasion with resiliency and soar. I could not stay down. I had to rise & chase my dreams. I completed a book.

Why does an author write? Why does anyone write? Why do I write? People write for all kinds of reasons, whether it be passion, talent, fun, to relate to, or to reach out to an audience. "I" write to "speak" to the mind a certain way, & I write to make people think... that is why I do things in my writings like BEAUTIFUL, & "she" is so...beautiful. When you pause or use capital letters, it creates a "feeling," like I just did with quotations. This is my writing style. I write for feeling, & I also write to help people think. So, I have written a book of inspirational quotes & reflections to help people with their daily struggles & give them a positive perspective on life.

Along the way of writing this year's worth of reflections, I showed my writings to others...many many others. They either liked it, loved it, found it interesting, & they never disagreed with it…but put their opinion in it. I did not mind. It is open for interpretation & feeling. In this book you may not notice, but I use the "&" sign & I believe there are no contractions. This is also "my" writing style that I chose to write. Also, through my journey of writing, I realized that I was writing around 5 central themes: Life is…., life's lessons, love & true love, music & dance, & God. Not all of this nation, these days, may appreciate God, but many believe in God or a higher power. For this, it is solely intended for positivity, & positivity goes a long way for many.

Moreover, people who have love taken away from them have so much more love to give. I have written from life's perspectives… outwardly & inwardly. Life reflected upon me, & I put it to clever use in inspirational writing. You cannot suppress love; it must be given openly, freely, & selflessly. We all have something at which we are good. For me, I hope my gift lies in writing. For you, I hope this book helps you to see something, anything good, because the world holds so much good than bad. I firmly believe this. So, to the audience... I thank you, wish you the best in this book, & once again, the motto of this book is "Cheers! Journey Well & God Bless." ---J.M.P.

NEW YEAR'S:
MY NEW YEAR'S WISH TO FRIENDS:

January 1st

"Here is to the New Year & everyone in it! May your year be great, fun, & enjoyable. I wish everyone the best of these ten things: love, happiness, laughter, fun, joy, excitement, passion, faith, amazing times, & hope. 'My' top ten are: peace, love, life, laughter, respect, dance, music, God, family, & friendship. Happy New Year everyone. Cheers & Journey Well."

January 2nd

"Life is all about choices. You choose what you live, & you live what you choose."

January 3rd

"Live life & never let life live you."

January 4th

"The heart can be bright...but you are the only one that can keep the light from going dim."

January 5th

"Your heart's choices make your life bright. It is connected spiritually. Only you can keep your heart from going dim & live what you may choose. Never let life control the light of your heart or become suffocated. Do not worry or falter. Just let your inner beauty shine outwardly. Let your heart breathe. It will see clarity because your heart is never opaque. It sees as it knows vision & is forever wisely wayward towards the correct path. Just trust, believe, & have faith in your heart in the same manner as you are breathing now."

January 6th

"Why reach down to tie your shoes when you can look up &
kick the day in the FACE!!!"

January 7th

"You have to manifest love because positive energy is bliss."

January 8th

"Life is a present full of surprises to open. While poised at this moment in life & time, you will find the guidance of a cavalier & navigated bright spirit. This spirit becomes the wind beneath your wings that wields & shapes the ability for you to take flight & fly freely with enthusiasm."

January 9th

"Do not be intimidated by beauty. Rather, be intimidated by success & failure because these two entities will bring you down, & if you are successful, then you will not fail. So, reach for the stars & soar like a caged butterfly."

"Our path is not something we look around for. Rather, it is placed at our feet. You must take a step forward, walk, & never base what is behind you on what is about to happen."

January 11th

"Dancing is how the soul sings, & singing is how the soul dances."

January 12th

"Beauty is rare. It takes a rare heart to notice & capture its glorious wonders. This notification is where the eye of the beholder ventures into splendor, passion, & love. Love is an adventure as life takes it under its wings & soars to Heaven. For love is a high like no other where inward beauty shines to its greatest potential, always knowing that purity is its best friend to astonish the eye of the beholder."

"Sometimes it is hard to find good things to do, but sometimes it is good to find hard things to do."

January 14th

"Life is FULL of memories... that is why you MUST make 'em! Do not use the past to predict the future but treasure EVERY moment because tomorrow may never come. So, you have to celebrate EVERY day! The past is there to help "today" remind us that YO!... We have lived, learned, & grown since then!!!"

January 15th

"A relationship can be like a roller coaster – up & down but a great ride! Sometimes, the great ride must end, but then again, it can be the ride of your life! Through these ups & downs along the way with screaming & hollering… you learn that the ride is not so bad. Is it? You hold on tightly to the one next to you & never want to get off!"

"When it comes to courage… you have to do it with a positive & keen vision, not knowing the outcome at the end of that tunnel. No matter how detrimentally dangerous the end of that tunnel may be… you must just do it."

January 17th

"You can take the man out of the boy... but you can never take the boy out of the man (same for a girl & a woman)."

January 18th

"Life is a ride – get on it, do not wait, & have a BLAST at the same time!!!"

January 19th

"Time comes & time goes. Good times come, & somehow, an enjoyable time just blindly flies by like a train. Valued times hold substance that never dies. Your heart is a memory – a vault that sustains, supports, & contains this valued substance of gold of memories in which these times hold. These times may pass you chronologically but are locked... eternally, safely, inescapable, & unforgettably within you, making you whole. It then shapes you physically, emotionally, mentally, & spiritually."

"They say, 'Do the kindest things in the kindest of ways.' When you do this, people become so much more humbled. Yet, why does it take this? Perspective is huge, yes, & what I have seen is that when you have 'a light' about yourself… people love your happy energy. So, stay humbled, patient, joyful, kind, lit, & always try to do the right thing. Because when you do, you will be richly rewarded through God & the universe in a universal way."

January 21st

"Try not to be about something you are not about."

January 22nd

"Music has no age. That is why good music never dies."

"Where is she? I am him. She is she. When will we be a 'we?' I wait patiently. Until that time comes… I will have fun. Until she & I become one... I will wait under the sun & dance under the moonlight, waiting for a romantic twilight. She will come, & I will embrace her, face her, taste her, & make her mine, but until then... I wait for our hearts to intertwine, & God… PLEASE let her find her path to mine!!!"

January 24th

"I do not know how to dance... I just move my feet & they take me where I need to go."

January 25th

"Two Words: Music Talks."

"They say good things come to those who wait... I have also heard good things take time & 'great' things happen all at once from the movie *Rat Race*. I say the good people who deserve the wait receive great things."

January 27th

"Stay strong. Never stray away from your blessings. Count them daily. Someone always has it worse. Knowing yourself is a PLUS! Many people go through life lost; you are not. I believe in you. Believe in yourself. Your friends do. Life is what you make it, how you let it affect you, how you face adversity, & resiliency is bliss. Bounce back & work on your weaknesses. Improve. Grow. Adapt. You are your best weapon of choice when it comes to life's battles. Create anything positive. Your vision – be thankful you can see it. Relax. Breathe. Meditate & move on. Every day is a new day, a clean slate. You have this. If your vision is bad, there must be a way to help it. A medical friend who is a nurse or doctor – even they can help you. Give love to yourself & help yourself. Being lonely is not a weakness; it is a strength. One thing I have learned lately is to fall in love with yourself. Pray & hope it gets better. It will be because the secret to life is positive energy produces positive results. Negative energy produces negative results. Negate from negativity. Stay positive always & the best results will come your way if you manifest it. May you have peace, joy, enthusiasm, hope, & belief in yourself... you got this. Finally, trusting God could be a task, or believing in Him. Put your 'love' into him versus trust. Hope, belief, & faith will do the rest. Cheers, Journey Well, & God Bless."

31

January 28th

"Here is to living it up, doing it up, & never giving up until the day we ALL go up!!!"

January 29th

"Like hippies from the 60s or 70s & shirts with tie-dye...
YES... our worlds were meant to collide!!!"

"Life is a strife. Cut it with a knife & say I am my own day. 'I' make 'MY' day! Today... I will live for what 'I' give today because that is ALL 'I' can do & I will stay true to today. Tell yourself that I have learned from 'my' life bookshelf, the ones 'I' love, the one above, & through 'that' 'MY' life is 'MY' knife. Cut life away."

January 31st

"When life gives you lemons, you make lemonade, limoncello vodka, lemon meringue pie, lemon bars, lemon cakes, lemon sherbet, lemon water, lemon pudding, lemon curd, fried lemons, lemon pepper chicken, lemon pepper pasta, lemon muffins, & remember that life IS abundant!"

FEBRUARY LOVE QUOTES
(FEB 1ST – FEB. 14TH)

"I am a firm believer that 'bad things fall apart, so good things can come together.' This is from the movie *Rat Race*. That is why I am so faithful in that all the bad that we have had… the only thing that could happen is greatness, & it is called "true love."

"To be held is why she yelled… to scream about, to dream about the one; the forgotten one. It was him hidden from her when she looked up into his eyes, like into the skies, seeing stars to heal her heart. It became clear he was now nearby. She had no reason to have yelled because now it was him in his arms. She was being held as she smiled all the while."

February 3rd

"The 3 Valuable L's of LIFE"

Love, Loss, & Learn

We have all loved something or someone valuable.

We have all lost something or someone valuable. &...

We have all learned from something or someone valuable."

"Love is a spiritual blue flame ignited universally deep within us buried down into the crevices of our souls, ready to burst out at any given moment. It is our choice to kindle the bonfire of passion & give in to the splendor of love when it sees & finds us like the romantic twilight of the moonlit, starlight, star-bright night sky that always does."

February 5th

"Love is beautiful. It is the only thing stronger than fear, hate, & anger. It travels throughout this world to the universe effortlessly… endlessly beautifully touching everything in its path with absolute beauty as well as grace from the Heavens to the skies, to Earth, & everyone, bringing absolute joy to our hearts. Love... what an amazing gift."

February 6th

"Every man has a dog in him. It is up to him whether to bark or bite or show love & affection, just like every woman has a cat in her. It is up to her whether to come up to you, claw at you, run away, love you, or show affection."

"When someone sees you for what you are worth, it is far more valuable than any piece of land, money, or materialistic thing, whether it be family, a friend, a coworker, a teacher, or even a lover. Love is real."

"Life is way too short to waste any time at all. You are only young once. Life is an adventure… so make more memories to look back on. They look back at the adventures they could have had while they could be out right now celebrating. You always want to feel young. A woman loves a man who keeps her young. The good nights & days that you live, whatever, those are the days that make you feel young when you love, live, & laugh in the moment. When you find someone with whom you can share these things… well then, my friend, do not ever let that go. Do not ever give up without a fight. To hell with anybody who makes you feel like you are ordinary! When you find this person, this rare, special-unique person… hold tight, & do not ever let them go. It rarely happens & you will know it because it is when you feel most alive! It can be a sappy world, no joke! All jokes set aside; it can be a "happy world"… if you choose to see it that way. You can be happy if you want to be. Have fun. Laugh until your belly hurts. Try foods that may seem weird. Make a bucket list. Have a conversation with an elderly person because they will always be wiser than you & teach you something new. Travel as much as possible because there is no telling what may happen that may surprise you. Love. Be happy... always. Live, love, & laugh life. Just let go. Free yourself with happiness. Fly away, & never float."

"Love someone for who they already are, what they already are, & what they already have become. Perfection is never guaranteed, but imperfections are loved easily. Love requires no remedy… just constant acceptance without approval. It is who & what we already are, & knowing this goes miles beyond recognition because the heart tells the eyes what the brain should already know supremely & soothingly."

"There is a connection in this universe that exists, that when felt is electric, and you have no control over. Just go with it, flow with it, & grow with it because it may never come again. This life may just blindly pass you by like a train whistling by you. It will be a moment, & at that moment, you must own it but remain calm & gravity will take care of the rest. The best will shine for the rest of your talented potential, & the rest of your love is nothing but exponential."

February 11th

"I notice the comforts in life that pass my way & make me stop in the tracks of my "train stop in this ride of life." I see the women who crumble in their hearts because they could never have kids. I see the old men in the parks who sit on a park bench because they lost their forever one & only… they know they will never find one that comes a fraction of a chance closer. I notice women stuck in the wrong relationships who do not know how to get out but keep going because they think they are in love. I notice all the children who fall to the ground so innocently, happily, looking up to the sky, & get right back up because they have not done that before. It is new to them, & because they do not know anything else but to get right back up, it is so easy & ecstatic for them.

I also notice all of the love that people give that goes unnoticed, like people letting you go first in traffic, people dancing & singing randomly in a happy demeanor, the best-unexpected surprises at the most unexpected moments, the sudden bursts of laughs given at the saddest moments of tears, 80-year old couples holding hands, couples holding hands in movie theatres & other public places, children playing in parks, & couples suddenly kissing each other all so happily as if no one is watching with a cavalier attitude. There are sudden outbursts of laughter out of nowhere in a movie theatre when no one else is even laughing. I notice the dogs & cats we see that bring us immediate joy & other animals too; the unexpected things that grasp us in nature, & most of all, the signs & symbolism that God gives us. He tells us… "You know what… how do you like the love I

47

have given to you on this blessed earth? How do you like My sense of humor? I love you so much, & I will never stop showing you My love & comforting you in life on your smooth train ride." Keep on riding because love is everywhere on these train tracks of love in this ride of life."

February 12th

"Hatred is what love will truly never know, & love is what hatred tries very hard to get ahold of."

February 13th

"Every great romance has a great love story."

VALENTINE'S DAY
REFLECTION

February 14th

"Love is a blessing. It is sometimes disguised, sometimes a surprise, & sometimes takes time. At best, it opens the eyes fully & is a true miracle. So wonderful is the gift of love. We all want love."

February 15th

"There are some things that will stick to you for a lifetime...
whether it be hurt, pain, vile, or hatred. Sin is everywhere
universally. Love, be happy, be thankful, & be thoughtful of
your surroundings. Praise God, & the universe... this is the
biggest gift one can receive. Stay blessed & manifest."

February 16th

"Love is the trailer of a savoir-faire driven life."

"Do we work for money, survival, or passion? If we work for money, then eventually, we will end up complaining. If we work for survival, then we are slaves. If you work for passion, then you love your job, & you never work a day in your life. Strive to work for passion so that you love what you do & are happy about what you do."

"An elephant cannot fly... meaning we are not supposed to be doing what we are not supposed to be doing. We are all built a certain way, & if we are not happy at the end of the day, then what are we living for? Fly like *Dumbo*."

February 19th

"Life is beautiful… captivate it!!!"

"Hope is the only thing that is more powerful than anger, hate, or fear. It is equal to love. It is an enormously powerful thing to hold onto. You either have it or you do not. So, if you have this powerful gift… hold onto hope & never let it go."

"Life is not easy. Life is about how you face adversity, perspective, & how you let it affect you. You have a choice to fall or rise. Hopefully, you can... soar!!!"

"Whatever you are doing has an outcome. So, be good at what you do today so you can be great at what you do tomorrow."

"Speak to someone wise. Speak to the elderly. Speak to someone cheerful. Ignore negativity. Make love & live in the moment, always."

"A lake is at peace when it is not disturbed. A tree stands still when the wind does not blow it. A candle's flame is still if not touched. One thing to keep in life is balance... the light within the dark, the hard within the soft, but do not forget about the in-betweens. Within the mediums is where you find your most balanced place of peace. Try striving for perfection to find your medium – your inner peace."

February 25th

"It may take a village to raise a child, but it takes a country to change America."

"We are always students in life. There is always something to learn in life, & there is always something we can gain for ourselves in this life."

"The reason you realize the difference between action & inability is because you embrace the fact of knowing & feel that thought of consciousness. Thus, a change happens as you do as well."

February 28th

"This is why we write – to be timeless, to make people think, to create FEELING... & to be different. Oh, to write is to touch what cannot be touched but felt & imagined."

LEAP YEAR DAY

February 29th

"Time passes us by like a train just whistling away. What we do with our time is up to us. Whether it happens during the days, weeks, months, or even every four years on a day like this... it can always become "your day." Make your day count... every day."

MARCH

March 1st

"When you speak my heart… I know that you know me."

"I have learned that what you see inwardly of yourself is not what others see outwardly, and vice versa."

March 3rd

"Unconditional love is something that, when given & felt, makes you say to someone, 'You do not even realize what you did (Eminem)... but I thank you for what I have been longing for this entire time.' This miraculous gift is something in which you accept me for everything I am, & it is beautiful, wonderful, & the best gift... ever."

"They say when one soul finds its soul mate, it knows. It might deny, lose faith, or not trust, but it knows. I know, I accept with a smile, & my heart is teaching my head to trust you… my soul mate."

ONE DAY

March 5th

"One day, someone may bring you flowers. Then, what is your worth? Are you still worth the same as you were before? Or are you worth more because that person sees the beauty that you possess? One day, you will realize that the mistakes you made then do not matter now because you are not perfect… but beautiful. The ones you will make in the future will not matter because you will have lived, learned, & grown immensely since then. One day, a fire will light inside you & ignite. It will burn & feed you a passion that makes you hungry & never want to stop… this is called love. One day, you will love. It will cause you to never stop giving to that one who makes you happy just because, & that person will do anything he can 'just' to make you smile. He will never make you cry. He will make you happy because he loves you from the depths & cavities of his soul. One day, you will be old & wrinkled, sitting on your front porch, staring out into the distance with a gaze of pure wonder while rocking happily & peacefully on your rocking chair. You rock with ease as the cool, comforting wind chimes blow. You are happy as your grandchildren play & laugh, & your children could ask you, 'Mother, how have you maintained happiness for so long?' She will tell them, 'Love... it was love. Him... your grandfather... it was him that made "us"... he & I... "He" gave me... love. He made me happy & rescued "my" life with…love. "One Day."

72 "

SUCCESS

March 6th

"There is nothing in this life that can stop you from success, just stress.

What is stress? Is it something to be suppressed, or that makes you depressed?

Perhaps, yes, stress is this & has the means to press.

Set a goal in life. If you go through life without a goal or aim, then why live?

Purpose is what drives you into a category of life where you are, whether it be childhood, elementary years, adolescence, work, career, marriage, retirement, or wherever your place is in time that you are arriving destination-wise in your pursuit of joy.

They say, 'Success is not measured by what you accomplish but by how far you have come to get there.' I say success is measured not by the length of time it took you to get there but by seeing how much heart & passion has produced a glorious result through repeated effort & discipline.

Too many people let themselves get knocked down for too many reasons. Succeed for yourself. Find success within yourself. Know that success & capabilities reside within you because you have the freedom and will to pursue what you want, & are free from burdens that try to bring you down & cloud your mind. Think clearly. See clearly. Do not let the mind cloud your vision or heart. Fight. Be willing, stand tall, & be brave. Love yourself. Know that anything is possible.

This life is yours, & you are free to make your own choices. Live freely. Love freely. Succeed & find purpose in this life. Aim for victory. Find a balance so that you may have equilibrium, rest peacefully in your comfort zone, live fluidly, breathe freely, openly, & happily."

March 7ᵗʰ

"When an action is done, do not let that action go untold…
meaning communication is 'always' key in life, wherever
you go, whatever you do, & whoever you are with."

"Some things are right. Some things are wrong. Some things should be left alone. Do you truly have to understand everything? Some things we misunderstand. Knowledge is power, indeed, but why try to understand everything? Live for the moment. Know now for the present. Swim in the present. Dance for tomorrow. Dream for the future. Sing for your troubles. Rejoice for peace & break sorrows. Embrace & treasure hugs. Do not pass up a kiss, a smile, or a laugh. Believe in love, & it will destroy evil. Listen to your heart. Voice your opinion, but be mindful of who is listening. Be a leader... NOT a follower! Compromise the facts. Dramatize reality with fun because vivaciousness is a play at heart for the wicked but young & the restless! Know that the older will ALWAYS be wiser than you! Remember the good times, for they may never come again. History is here for a reason… that is why it 'was' written. You are only young once. Life is an adventure… so make many great memories to hold on to. Have fun. Laugh until your belly hurts. Try foods that may seem weird. Make a bucket list. Have a conversation with an elderly person because they will always be wiser than you & will teach you something new. Travel as much as possible because there is no telling what may happen that may surprise you along the way. Love. Be happy... always. Live, love, & laugh life. My point to the amazing advocates out there is that if you have not found love yet, or even at all… then I challenge you dearly to seek it. Love is too priceless to forsake this God-given gift. If you do not find this gift, then you will never understand what is misunderstood, what is right, or what is wrong… because it is love that makes everything right but never wrong. It will

NEVER be misunderstood! With love… NOTHING, & I do mean NOTHING, you beautiful people & rare, captivating souls out there… NOTHING can go wrong! So, I dare ANYONE to wrong themselves… with love."

March 9th

"Tell someone this… I am as smart as much as you think I am dumb."

March 10th

"You never know someone or something until you are in the exact situation. Avoid prejudices & judgmental notions as failure is one of life's biggest lessons to learn from."

"It is better to think two steps ahead instead of being two steps behind. This is how winning is achieved. This is vital for success, & perhaps even imperative for yourself."

March 12th

"If you can look at your life & see, feel, & know that you are doing something wrong, then you are doing something right. If five years from now, you have learned from those mistakes & grown, then that, my friend… is a beautiful life lesson. You deserve a pat on the back. In fact, reward yourself for that, & celebrate for it."

"Life is so much better when looking at a baby. Nothing compares to a baby or lights up the world like a baby."

March 14th

"Life is a spark. In this life, a person is a spark. Their flame never goes out. When they pass from this realm, their flame carries on. Do not let your heart let its flame go out. Rather, carry on their spirit, the spark that they have passed onto you, & ignite them to others. For they would want a bonfire to be lit in the children of their name!"

March 15th

"Love is who you are; love is all that you hopefully know. Love is a journey, an untraveled, & unfinished road. Love is all you must show. You have come from a place where you were beaten down, & love was taken away from you… but those who have love taken away from them... have so much more love to give. So, choose to rise, choose to soar, & when you knock on a certain door... Heaven will be raining on the ones who brought you down like never before."

"G.R.A.C.E. ... Great Renditions Around Us that Create Empowerment."

"We are all built a special way when it comes to talking to people... like a house. We can show them any door we want to or open any window, & we can even kick them out the back door. We can tear down our walls or even show them all the beautiful rooms we want to show them. We can let them into any room we want because it is our house to show them. It is our house of conversation; we are inviting them into our lives to show them all the rooms of our beautiful 'home of conversation.' We can even sit on the roof & stare at the stars with them, or we can even sit on the 'porch of conversation' listening to wind chimes of life as they speak their soul to us. So, enjoy talking to people because their home is your home of conversation, & there is no telling how beautiful their rooms are."

March 18th

"The one who loves the most does not receive love. The one who gives the most does not receive what is supposed to be given. The one for whom one cares most does not get cared for. The one who is kindest does not meet their kindred spirit. The one who is most free does not get freed. So, they wait, as their shadow of love is out there, & they wait in despair, hoping for their angel to rescue them from their long-awaited love nightmare. Stay hopeful, for your angel will come."

March 19th

"Life is splendid splendor. It is all about how you spend it. Savor the flavor of life."

March 20th

"Has every story been told? Has every song been sung? Has every painting been painted? When it is your story, your song, & your painting… it becomes real and magical & it relates to you. Remember that music, art, & love travel through this world to touch, inspire, & relate to you. So, when you see it, hear it, & feel it, love the magic of it because it is your story. It will always be meant for you at that place & time, friend. Journey well with this amazing gift of what art, music, & love have to offer you."

March 21st

"If you can do one thing in this life, leave a legacy of yourself on life's own bookshelf."

March 22nd

"Say, 'I know it will be alright in rain, snow, hail, or shine!'
Put the past behind. We cannot fast forward or rewind. We
cannot pause. We cannot fight the good fight unless it needs
fighting, & we can shine good lighting on the subject & help
someone never forget that they still have a strong mindset.
We can love to live our life for our wife. We can keep the
spark alive & stray from strife. We know that through all our
trials & tribulations, we will still show appreciation. We will
stand tall above all when someone tries to break down our
wall, & we know it will always be all right, rain, snow, hail,
or shine, because we know how to shine every day."

"This life is full of curveballs, surprises, speed bumps, & roadblocks. Expect the unexpected. Fifty percent of this life is directed at you, & fifty percent of this life is not directed at you. So, with these unexpected curveballs, surprises, speed bumps, & roadblocks, knowing that all this can happen, always make the best of it because your life can be gone in an instant. Visit family, friends, & loved ones while you can. Make your bed daily & tip your servers. Make memories to look back on because treasured moments are sacred, & when unexpected surprises become treasured moments… life becomes special in the utmost of ways when life hands you the moments right in your path. Make memories last, always, & be happy as much as possible."

March 24th

"Love is hard, but so is life. Life is not easy, but neither is love. L.O.V.E. – Living Overly Vulnerable & Evolving. L.I.F.E. – Loving with Insight Fully for Everyone. If you live to love, love to live, & are not happy at the end of the day, then that is all that really matters because if we are not happy at the end of the day & evolving with insight, then what are we living & loving for? Get busy living. Get busy loving. Get busy Evolving. Grow. Love. Live."

March 25th

"From the 20s, 30s, 40s, 50s, 60s, 70s, 80s, 90s, to 2000s, it was bound to happen – a free spirit… do you feel it? Driving around town, from uptown to downtown, with the windows down, cool wind in our hair with not a worry or care… say, 'I know it will be alright… rain, snow, hail, or shine! I will put the past behind me!' The happiest people live in the present, so open this gift, & feel it. To all you free spirits from every generation, show appreciation, live in the present because it is such a happy feeling, so free, & are meant to be free!!!"

March 26th

"If you are going to have an ego, have a 'healthy ego'… meaning be confident in what you do because overconfidence can be a weakness. No one likes egotistical, arrogant people with too much pride. It crosses boundaries that do not need to be crossed. Aggression occurs, you lose control, & you lose sight of who you are. So, have a healthy ego, be confident, & have pride in what you do, beautifully, in a healthy way & people will love you for it."

"Anytime you see negativity…you should crumble it into a ball, shove it in a corner, & keep it against that faraway wall. Surround yourself with nothing but positivity because we are all creators in this place & life. The time to do something is now because positive energy produces positive results, & negative energy produces negative results. So, surround yourself with positivity always, do you, & you will even surprise yourself as a creator."

March 28th

"If you ever say that you are not good at something or are not good at anything, then that is not true. We are all good or talented at something. We just must look inside ourselves & ask ourselves what it is. It could be hiking, carpentry, psychology, helping a friend, cooking, or whatever it may be; we are ALL good at something! Just ask yourself, 'What am I good at?' Then soar, do it, & have fun with it because the time to do it is now!!! Nike it!"

"Your life can become interesting at the flip of a switch in just 5 minutes or even 5 seconds. So, make the best of it. Make it fun. Make it better. Make it perfect & make it interesting if you can. Pick & choose your battles. Whatever you do, make the situation interesting, fun, & the best you can of it, whatever the moment may be."

"True, real, & smart fighters – the best fighters – never swing first. The trained ones finish it quickly. They strike at places & parts of the body intricately & in a tactical way that the other person does not even see coming. When it is over fluidly & fluently with rhythm, timing, & a springboard effect… the opponent will never mess with you again because they know that you are a force to be reckoned with, & revenge is a hole that they will never fill."

March 31st

"Great families & friends think alike."

APRIL

April 1st

"It can be a total surprise when you realize total self-growth, self-discipline, & self-worth. So always grow & know that you are always a student in this life. Blossom, flourish, & spread yourself into what you truly are inside & out because if you just do you, you will surprise & even, at times, amaze yourself."

April 2nd

"Reality is never meant to be feared. It is only feared because fear has been fed into the mind from whatever outer sources & whatever was in the mind 'before' fear... 'that'... is reality."

April 3rd

"Kids are like technology... they never stand still. So stay updated on your electronics, guys."

"There are 168 hours in a week & 10,080 minutes in a week. So, the next time you tell someone you do not have time for them, & you cannot take 5, 10, or even 20 minutes out of your day or week for them, think about this... it is not that you do not have time – it is the fact that you, yourself, do not, will not, & cannot make or allow yourself to spend time on or with this person. It is your fault because you conflict yourself with the time that you have created against yourself. Selfishness exists so much in this world, & selfishness is not necessarily a bad word. People get so offended when they hear this word without knowing the 'true meaning' of the word 'selfish.' It means to take care and self-care of one's wants & needs. Yet, when it comes to the point where you constantly put 'yourself' before 'others,' then it becomes a 'problem.' Become selfless with your time, & free yourself from the conflict within."

April 5th

"Every crazy has genius. There is chaos in genius & order in chaos."

April 6th

"This world is full of amazing things we either understand or do not understand. The thirst for knowledge is there. Do we care or not care? Is there air or no air? To question is only human & logical. To not question is for the lost & illogical. We are in a society where people want to stick out & are full of rebels. So, question anyone & anything because the answer may surprise you, & the idea of knowing is bliss."

"A crook with a crooked smile in the most devilish of ways, with the spirit of an angel & a heart of gold, is someone who is mischievous in this swift breeze of a fresh breath of air in this life, & the only crime they could commit is theft to one's heart & soul of love in a ghost-town of a lonely heart."

"Life can really beat you down & tear you apart. Some words are created to scare you. Winning is only half the battle. The road to recovery is half the success, so I say hello there, the angel to my nightmare. You are the beacon of light that shines hope from a faraway land in a not-so-distant place close to my heart that I have needed for a long time. Like a soldier who has fallen in battle, I rise, breathe in clean air, & you rescue me… because I know that with the right vision, nothing will ever keep me from failing in this life so long as I have you, the sacred angel from my nightmare."

April 9th

"Anyone can have a good time, naturally. Existing is living. It is who we have always been since birth, who we still are, & who we will always be. Pity for anyone who needs a drink for their sorrows, smoke to escape, or a drug to help them get high & feel better. When we were children, we knew exactly how to be happy without any of these things. We should remember those times, & act on this naturally because it is who we have always been since birth. Substances we need to be happy are love, laughter, & life. These things have always occurred in us & through our bodies naturally. Alcohol & drugs were never a part of our bodies in the beginning."

April 10th

"Thoughts become beautiful when they leave the lips & pen. It is important to say or write our thoughts and share our experiences. Often, when we do that, it transforms our thoughts into something bigger and more empowering. Love is so messy, wild, as well as strong, but it is so sacred & delicate at the same time. It comes in, steals our breath, & changes us altogether... for the better."

April 11th

"Some songs are meant to be just listened to. For example, the beating heart of your lover, the roaring & clapping of an enthusiastic crowd, or even the soothing waves of the beautiful, serene, calm ocean. It brings warmth, depth, & energy to the depths & cavities of your captivating heart, mind, body, spirit, & soul."

April 12th

"The thing about being a fighter is we do not want to hurt you. We all fight hard, love harder, & protect even more. So, keep fighting, loving hard, & protecting the ones you love."

April 13th

"Intelligence is meant to be challenged, for if it were not... then we might all seem like idiots."

April 14th

"Just when you think everything is fine, dandy, & perfectly going your way – the world throws you a wild card."

April 15th

"Put your hand up if you have ever met someone & you find yourself often wondering what they are doing randomly during the day."

April 16th

"Time is timeless. There is no 'late.' Everything is happening as it is supposed to, so rejoice in the loving arms of time because time is 'with you' and not 'against you.' Never hurry for the struggle because it is not worth stressing over time & conflicting yourself with the concept of time. Love time, for it is in time that time does not exist."

April 17th

"To be or not to be, huh? How about to see or not to see? THAT is the question! How open or closed-minded can people be, eh?"

April 18th

"The breath that we are breathing right now is the only one that matters."

April 19th

"Inspiration is a trail that leads to creative desire. It ignites wonder & fuels a light that only we see, surprising us in ways that, when accomplished, leave us amazed. In an awestruck moment… it transforms us, revealing abilities we didn't know we possessed – success, vision, confidence, relief, comfort, happiness, & love."

April 20th

"Time is a commodity we do not have an advantage of. Yes, we can make the best use of our time, of course. Yet, in the end, it may get the best of us."

"A school of fish feeds a man, the hunter-gatherer. Does a coin thrown in a jar feed a man sitting on the roadside holding a sign wanting work?"

April 22nd

"I know not of mechanics, but I can change a tire... just like a handicapped person who knows not of their legs but still climbs a mountain."

"We all fear something. It is a concept of the mind. Near something in the frontier of our mind, we accept it & leave it behind. We conquer it, divide it, rise above it, & to ashes, it will fall if you have & find that power & will to control it. So, seek it with strength. You are your own best weapon of choice. Now fight."

April 24th

"Do you understand what you do not understand? Do you know what you do not know? The unknown is the unknown. Knowledge is power, indeed, so why try to understand everything? Some people thrive on wanting to know. Why? It eats them. Know that it is okay "not to know." It really is okay not to know everything. You know why? Because life is going to unfold how it is going to unfold. It is not in your grasp, & it is not in your control. So, the next time you want to ask why, stop & try to think for yourself, even laugh. Ignoring something is a sign of intelligence. Because sometimes some things are better left misunderstood, & this life loves to surprise you in the best of ways. It will reward you if you let it. What I mean by that is that it is in giving yourself to others your love that you get back gifts of beauty from other entities."

"We have heard the clichés: life is what you MAKE it, it is what it IS, life is about CHOICES... so here, it IS not a race thing unless you CHOOSE to MAKE it a race thing. You have a choice every day to choose what your life is, to be wise in every action you choose, so make your choices something good & wise when creating & indulging in a conversation about ethnicity, diversity, & culture."

April 26th

"This life is one of circumstances, choices, & conclusions. It is up to you where to draw your line, use wisdom, & make your decisions."

"Like a rebel, my outlaw heart was born to love, be a thief & steal my heart. Lie in my arms & cheat death. Put me to the test, & I will succeed because an angel will save me when it comes to the arms of loneliness that will rescue me from darkness & cleanse me, for I know how capable & strong I am when it comes to love. So, I set out to this frontier & rebel my heart to win over the heart of an angel's wings of beauty to rescue me because I know she is out there for me to fill me with her grace, beauty, & abundance of love."

"Some people do things out of spite with might. Why try to fight when there is no light? Some act on impulse. It is so easy to act on impulse when you feel that your pulse is so high, no lie. Yet, when you act out of love for the ones you care about – these are the best acts, true facts because they will always love you back for this, true bliss & redundant, they will thank you with abundant open arms."

"In my eyes, there are 3 types of people... the ones who speak up, the ones who do not, & the ones who want to but will not."

April 30th

"Imagination – some really have it, some can have it, so come with me... look up to the stars, & think that out of every star out there, each one has a system of its own. Journey into a land of life & love where there is no racism. The power to imagine is bliss. Think beyond math & science. The possibilities are endless: music, movies, food, cars, art, culture, the ancient world, spirituality, mystery, space, freedom... the beyond. We see how things work, what exists, what does not, what can, what will, what is, & what is not, what is understood, & what is misunderstood. Freedom of the mind is all yours! Oh, to imagine & dream is to adventure out in your mind to destinations, creations, & cultivations in a beautiful way so that expression becomes a part of you. You take it & make something of it into a mold that becomes a part of you that constructs a creative concept that just makes you feel good. This feeling is where the heart of inspiration flows, goes, shows, & glows. So, imagine! It is the best vacation that leads you to the best places of your enthusiastic, loving, & beautiful mind!!!"

131

MAY

May 1st

"Listen to the beat of your heart, the melody of life, dance to the rhythm of your soul, & tune in to the tempo of your mind."

"You cannot base behavior on principle because behavior is not constant. There is hope, change, & love that proves this."

"Some people you meet, you have met, & they are set. Some people you just get. Then there are those people... you know those people; they are the ones you never regret or forget."

May 4th

"Hope is fear's luminous ally that waits in the whims of destruction, waiting to light the way. Now is the breath of hunger staying wayward on your path."

May 5th

"You are the only version of yourself in which you are designed & destined to be you."

"Find the compassion of your dreams. It will be right within the reach of your fingertips."

May 7th

"We all have a direction in this life. So, let yourself reflect on what you can be for your best reflection. Feed off other's energy as they are infectious to be around. The vibrations that they, we, or you & I can emit that feel good are the ones worth being around. When you know something is negative, crumble it, throw it into a ball, shove it into a corner, & move on. Keep nothing but positivity around you. When you feel good or even great or even wonderful, so does everyone around you, so maintain a vibrant & upbeat outlook. Laughter, smiles, & happiness are what make life worth living, dreaming about, and experiencing. Engage in good & friendly conversations. Try & eat well. Go to places that feel amazing. Walk through this life like it is the best ride you are taking every day. Seek out whatever makes you feel the best when you are at the pinnacle of joy because nothing can bring you down when you are at your best. Be your cavalier spirit, one who will brighten up all who surround you. Marvel this notion. Now go, light that fuel of joy, stay hungry, stay eager, & do not retire what makes you the happiest, beautiful & rare, captivating souls out there that you are."

May 8th

"You cannot use the past to predict the future or think about the what ifs in life. Rather, live in the present. That is why it is called "a gift." If we are not living, laughing, loving, or smiling… then what are we living for? Get busy dying or get living."

May 9th

"Live, laugh, & love. Wine, dine, & have a fun time."

May 10th

"In this life, we must open ourselves up like the gift we are. We all have a gift that we must spiritually uplift. So, show & glow what you know."

"Once a spark is lit, it is too lit to quit. The question is, does it fit? What is meant to be is meant to be. So, by God, let what is meant to be, be."

"It is so powerful that an idea, a dream, a goal, love, happiness, prayer, focus, meditation, hope, faith, belief, & God together can make you anything you want to be. As a directed, guided, & purposeful individual in this lifetime… you can conquer anything you want to."

May 13th

"Treasure the good moments that happen in life because they are the best ones that last forever in the heart, mind, body, & soul."

"Life is funny. You never know what is smiling your way…
so laugh, dance, & embrace life until your face never has a
chance to catch the taste of fate."

SUCCESS

May 15th

"Life has many things. One thing I have learned is that it is not about how many times you have fallen but rather how many times you rise. Success is measured by what we have become & how far we have come along to get where we are today. I listened to three songs today: "King of Wishful Thinking," "How to Save a Life," & "Failure Is Not Flattering." Wishful thinking is a deathtrap; it will quickly put you in quicksand, & it will get you nowhere fast. Thinking you can do something is one thing. "Knowing" you "will" do "any" thing & "everything" in your will to succeed is bliss. Yoda from Star Wars Episode V of Empire Strikes Back said, "Do or do not. There is no try." That is a way of life. You can only save your own life. God can too. Parents, friends, co-workers, and lovers are there to aid & guide you, but you are your own tool of destiny, survival, & fight in life. Life is an opportunity. Seize it & save it yourself. Do not watch it. Sail it & fly away. Failure is not flattering. It happens, yes, & everyone has failed at something, but it is our mistakes that mold us into success & shape us into the clay that sculpts us into the better beings we are today. Our past does not dictate our future necessarily; rather, it makes us stronger every day because we see where we have been, & terrible things happen, of course. Remember, terrible things fall apart, so wonderful things come together, so amazing things can happen. My message is: rise always. Do not just "think" you can do something...ever. "Know" you can. "Believe" you can. Have "faith" that you can & you simply will. It really is that easy. Save your own life with

God & love. Do not let failure get the better of you because success is just at your fingertips. Bruce Lee said, "It is like a finger pointing at the moon. Do not look at the finger, or you will miss allllll of that Heavenly Glory." Success is all over the place. It is right in front of you. Just go now & seize it. This is just one of the many blessings of life that have been bestowed upon us from God... SUCCESS!!!"

"When you figure out that you can be yourselves around each other naturally & have so much fun, then that is the one to run with to the sun."

May 17th

"Love is timing, a place, & a face for the right person at the right time. Wait for fate & the perfect date. They will come along like a brand-new song, & you will smile all the while."

"Arguing is for the feeble-minded. Avoid it at all costs. Ignoring someone or something is a sign of intelligence. A bee will not sting unless you bother it."

"See the good in everything, & the bad around you will wonder why. Let them wonder because goodness astonishes the pessimistic."

May 20th

"You cannot fight fire with gasoline in life."

May 21st

"Life is a constant test & battle to see how far we can fall. So, rise, shove it in its face, & show it that you are stronger than the barriers that it tries to bring you down with. Soar, fly, breathe, spread your wings, succeed, & never float."

May 22nd

"Expect less & nothing more. Who knows? In the end, what you receive may be more."

"Love is a maze thing… is that why it is amazing? Yet why must it be a maze thing, though?"

May 24th

"You can only manage what you allow your mind to encompass."

May 25th

"Blue fires exist... empaths, who feel, fly fiercely as high as
the sky, do not lie, love, are peaceful as a dove from above,
are so true – these exquisite flames of blue."

May 26th

"It doesn't matter what you do or wear, how you wear your hair, what you do or say from day to day… tomorrow, if there's sorrow, you will always be beautiful every day very full."

May 27th

"As you get older, your friend circle shrinks, yes, but it expands into the "closeness" of who people are to you."

May 28th

"I hope you never lose your sense of curiosity
When you get a thrill from hearing music
Or move & groove
You will never stop its generosity
May you never underestimate one single note or beat
God forbid music ever leave your body or feet
I hope that one day, just one day,
You feel huge when you stand on that stage
Whenever the crowd roars & cheers, you unleash your
passion outside your inner cage
Promise me that you will give music & dance a fighting
chance
That you will belt out & sing
Like a singer's dream
& dance a dance floor
Like never before
With your free spirit, you will feel it
Liberate yourself when you
Celebrate music & dance for itself
& when you get the choice for people to hear your voice to
sing or
A glance for people to see your dance

Like a phenomenal romance...

I hope you sing, &
I hope you dance. (Inspired by the song 'I hope you
dance')"

May 29th

"Overconfidence is a sign of arrogance & is a weakness if used as arrogance. The key to self-confidence is overindulgence. Tell yourself, "I have been here before, & 'you' want to knock on 'my' door? I do not think so because this is my show. I got this because I cannot be dismissed. I am stronger than you, & I do not belong to you." Intimidation is your only limitation. Fly. Do not break or falter, alter, for anyone, no one, or even everyone. Stay true to yourself & do you for yourself. You got this like no one before or after you. Then look up, & all of a sudden have some laughter so true because this life offers you so many gifts that sometimes you just have to suddenly spiritually uplift what is so great about you."

May 30th

"People in life that you come across are your community; do you see? So, always look for the good in your neighborhood."

May 31st

"Life is a tapestry of a multitude of people who set a magnitude & whirlwind of fire within your heart & impact you with lighting. When they walk away, they do not leave. They imprint a signature that is eternally not abandoned creating an earthquake deep within the crevices of your heart & a tidal wave at your feet. You leave this life not in a natural disaster but rather in an enigma to be answered when you get to Heaven ecstatically."

JUNE

June 1st

"An artist's heart is easily inspired, never expired, never retired, & it is always in dire need of fire & always on fire."

June 2nd

"Signs are here, there, everywhere, & even in the air. Look in life's book to be taken & get shaken. It is a treasure, a pleasure, whenever, wherever you go, when life has something for you to show, something for you to know, that is important & fragrant. So, inhale, exhale, & smell. In fact, you will be able to tell because signs are all around blasting a sound to make things obvious to you & point you in the right direction & let you know what is right, giving you light, & insight with God's might."

June 3rd

"Life is my high, music is my crack, dancing is my ecstasy,
& singing is my tropical island. These are my drugs of life."

June 4th

"Rules are made to be followed, abided by, & broken because nothing is constant or perfect, & there is always change in a system."

"Hope is a great, wonderful, & beautiful thing to embrace. Sometimes I look up, wonder, & ask, "God... why are You so good to me?"

June 6th

"Love is a mystery that continually writes history making a heart a part of someone's world to be heard & begotten never forgotten. It comes into our lives & thrives giving us intensity. It shows us our destiny to whom we are meant to be with, stand by, support, fight for, never give up on, stay true to as well as loyal, make happy, & always fall in love with all over again with when it comes to the one that is our true love."

June 7th

"Life is full of curve balls & surprises- mysteries that open up treasure boxes that we have yet to discover."

June 8th

"A good picture is something that normally is not taken. A good quote is something that normally is not said. A good song is one that usually is not heard, & a good painting is something that you must try to figure out or do not understand so that one will. Art... it is the best expression of something you love, understand, & know. You will love it, you will understand it, you will know it... then again maybe you will not, & that is ok because this is the beauty of art."

June 9th

"You can break the law, but you can only break it how they want you to break it."

"Love me now, love me then, never forget me when you see me again now & then. One day, my day will come when you will not see me again. Visit me now so my memory is forever in your heart & spirit someway, somehow so when I see you thereafter, we can share laughter & smile all the while."

June 11th

"When God gives you a dance floor in life... you dance your life with all your heart like EVERYONE IS watching! Because the beat of your heart, sunshine, & glimmer of your smile can impact anyone who watches."

June 12th

"Do what is worth talking about & remembering… that way, when you talk about it, it will be accomplished & worth remembering instead of just talking about it like you were going to do something about it. Act. Do not talk about it."

June 13th

"Martial arts is a dance… you just have to know how, when,
& why to take the lead at the very precise moment."

June 14th

"If you think you have given up then you just simply have my friend, BUT... if you have not... then the journey can only & always have a beginning with a concrete end my friend."

MY FRIEND:

June 15th

"You are the light in the dark at the end of the tunnel when I begin to funnel, the lost when I cannot be found, the heartbeat when I have no sound, the best when I face a test, & the face of a place when I need grace. You are the inhibition to my exhibition in my life & strife. You are the smile when I have been lonely for a while, the advice when I am faced with my vice, an ear to listen so my heart can glisten, & someone to walk & talk with me so I do not have to worry about someone having to gawk at me. You are my vacation when I need a destination, my glad when mad, my happy when sappy, here to wipe away my tears & fears, a fame to make a game out of my shame, & a life in me when there is strife in me. You are my strength in me when I am weak, week after week, my fire of desire, my earthquake that makes me not quake but wake, the lightning that strikes me with wonder, & the thunder that humbles me with laughter. You are the stargaze in me when all I see is haze on my cloudy days. You are a beautiful means to an end when what I need most is always just you to be there… because you are always there when air is not there for me to fight & defend... My Friend."

"When God reveals something to you, is it providence or extravagance? Nothing is of extravagance when it comes to divine intervention. Something of such providence is the gift of light that He bears to us when we least expect it. Remember your third eye, stay open-minded, & be thankful for what is shown in these incandescent moments before they are moments of evanescence."

June 17th

"Music is THEE Best expression of emotional content in THEE utmost possible way!!!"

"A great spirit is not defined by how a person interacts necessarily with people, rather more delicately with "nature." Therefore, you can always tell the "nature" of a person, how, & why they have a great spirit."

June 19th

"Fear can be a powerful ally if wielded with the right force & in the right direction for the right cause."

"Life is a construct…with all the right parts & framework together, there is nothing that can destroy you."

June 21st

"Desire will never retire or expire. What you want you do not need, & what you need you do not want. If you want something, then forget it. If you need something, & it is for the right reason then get it. Remember, though, what you deserve... you will receive."

June 22nd

"Whether we all are simple or complicated… we are all created to coexist, & this cannot be resisted. We are all equal to become a life after a sequel. So, while we are here... we can at least try to be sincere."

"Love brings many trials & tribulations- happiness, tragedy, heartache, children, death... but to overcome all of these & still love, that is a gift. Marvel at the ones who hold love close & dear to their heart no matter what they go through. These are the ones who know & see life to its truest potential because life is not about sadness, heartache, or death. It is about living, love, happiness, & laughter. So, marvel at the ones who know how to be happy & love. It takes a special person to always love no matter what the situation is."

"We all fail in this life. Learning through humility is one's capability to realize that they have the ability, potential, & effort to learn with confidence. This confidence brings vision, clarity, focus, & the ability not to fail once they have seen & known what they have done wrong. With this vision, there is nothing left to do but succeed."

June 25th

"Sadden not your heart, dampen not your spirit, sharpen your mind, & kindle the fire that your body's desire will never retire. Stay strong."

June 26th

"When it happens from above, & you find true love... you tell them, "Thus, I look into your eyes & I see us. I see me & I see you. That is why I love you."

"Fear is the thief that tries to steal from the heart & mind. Do not let it trade off the values & morality that are set in your heart. It is like you are standing at the edge of a cliff, looking at the mountains ahead of you, wondering whether to jump or not. Only you can jump in the sky & skydive fearlessly. Fear is a concept in the mind that tries to manipulate you. Are you going to control it, or let it control you? There is no thief of the heart & mind when it comes to fear if you know how to control it. It is all a mindset; so, go from there, climb any mountain you want, stand at the edge of any cliff you want, & soar any sky you wish your heart & mind to."

June 28th

"Life is FULL of memories. That is why you MUST make them! Do not use the past to predict the future; treasure EVERY moment because tomorrow may never come. So, you got to celebrate EVERY day. The past is there to help "today" to remind us that YO... we have lived, learned & grown since then!!!"

June 29th

"Never underestimate yourself, for you could be your most powerful weapon."

June 30th

"They say girls never chase a boy, & boys never chase a girl. BUT if you are going to chase something in life, chase THESE top ten things... your dreams, inspirations, aspirations, dedication, devotion, loyalties, faith, desires, hope, & Above ALL, chase your HEART!!!"

JULY

"An old Indian proverb says, 'Behind every mountain is another mountain.' What I say is that behind that last mountain is a paradise of an exotic beach to rest ashore."

July 2nd

"Behind every bad boy is the nice guy, hopeful romantic standing on the sideline that the girls do not want."

July 3rd

"Every day, you get a clean slate to start a new one or a new day. This day or today is the best day between yesterday & tomorrow, which is "your" or "my" day. So, call it that, & make it whatever you want. Now go for it. You got this."

FOURTH OF JULY REFLECTION

July 4th

"It is amazing that fireworks were invented as early as 2,000 years ago, & to this day, they still cause amazement & wonder to the eye. Such a beauty the Chinese did; Happy Fourth, everyone."

July 5th

"Friends who care, when have time to spare, will always be there, & by not judging you, they will always care."

"There are times when you want to give up. You look at your life & you see everything right in front of you, like the horizon of the sea. You may want to throw it all away or keep on sailing. Things come into your mind that try to hold you down & clutter you. Tell it, Stop! No! Halt! Like a blockade, block it, & push it away like the tides. You are like the ocean… your emotions… calm, serene, & intent on achieving your positive emotions. Show devotion & keep on moving. Sail your ship & journey with calm steering. The horizon is just ahead, & the sea of life is yours to sail however you so desire. Sail freely, openly, & serenely."

July 7th

"If you are frowning- then you must be drowning because laughter is like smiling with styling & profiling."

July 8th

"When you give without any sense of reward, that is a humble heart. People who give without receiving know that they are doing their part. Giving does not require a thank you. The ones who give do not have to have a thank you, know what they do, & they know that what they are doing is that much true."

July 9th

"Love is all around us. It surrounds us. It heals us. It binds us. It penetrates us, & it hits us when we least expect it. Timing & placing happens when we least expect it… to look for it does no justice. Internationally & universally known as a God-given gift, priceless, & a miracle, it can be taken away but never forsaken. Be thankful that it is always around you. Know that God loves you & will always show it to you in the most mysterious of ways. Love the ones around you, for you never know how long they will be here, but the love that they have forever remains."

July 10th

"I love how the rain can take away pain, & noticing the serenity brings peace of plenty. The simple things in life take away strife. Come rain any day & always comfort the way."

"One of the ways you must grow in this life is to let go of your pride, admit fault, learn to apologize, & forgive. Without doing these things first in a critical emotional situation, you will never be the bigger person. It is not about being the bigger person. It is about doing the right thing from the heart truly, sincerely, & righteously from the heart. For the better good, you can serve God, family, friends, yourself, & others."

July 12th

"Forever Accepting Mistakes in Love Yearly…
F.A.M.I.L.Y."

July 13th

"S.S.E.A.T. Selfishness, sympathy, empathy, accountability, & trust. Take a "seat" & see that every day, it is hard to find people who are "selfless," sympathize, can sympathize so easily, & put themselves in someone else's shoes. Also, many people do not want to be held accountable for fault & cannot admit their wrongs. Trust is so huge. Every day, Americans are told the wrong thing. People lie in relationships, & it makes it harder & harder for us to trust each day. Try & become selfless, sympathize, empathize, be accountable, & take that risk to trust because good hearts do exist in this world every day right here, right now."

July 14th

"From the stars to the dirt love can hurt. From the Earth to the skies, it opens the eyes. Love feeds, needs, & stays for the days. It never leaves, but it makes us believe & helps us relieve. Like an oasis in a desert, it is as sweet as dessert. It never leaves us & is always constant. Like gravity, it pulls us together & intertwines like vines. It heals & appeals like a mystery, making history and presenting beautiful emotions with devotion. Stay forever & keep us together with this amazing feeling called love. We are forever in your debt as you commit theft to our hearts stealing away our truth. Beautiful you forever are & eternal. Love is never-ending & amazing. It is no wonder how much of a blessing you are. We are nothing but thankful for this beautiful & graceful gift dearly called love."

July 15th

"There are tears, fears, & laughter with the years, which are key to a long life, not strife. Live it & give it."

"Life is not complicated. Complicated people complicate life."

July 17th

"The word is perspective. Perspective is how you look at something & interpret a situation. This morning, I looked across my street & I saw my neighbor's yard. I saw great warm memories of my past that made me smile & brought joy to my heart as I let out laughter to myself. I was happy, not sad one bit. The past is who we are, where we come from, our background, & our foundation. From my perspective, I love my past because it made me the strong person I am today. If not for my past, I would not be the happy person I am today. True… not everyone has had a happy life, but that does not mean you cannot be happy today… does it? The past is just a building block that creates us. It does not define us. It just shows us how we can improve ourselves. If I was happy then, then why could I not be happy now? If you were sad then, can you be happy now? Happiness is a choice. You create your own happiness. So, find out what makes you happy because it is not in the past… it is how you look at anything in a certain way in a positive manner & figure out how to make the best creation of that moment & go from there right here at this moment, right now."

"Dealing with emotions is an everyday thing. Knowing them is a skill. Recognizing them is a talent. Utilizing them to your advantage by interpreting them into knowledge & an information superhighway that shouts at you easily emotionally, mentally, & spiritually to teach you that what is going on around you is a gift. Lastly, knowing when & how to not let them affect you is something that can be taught through life's lessons, is unbelievably valuable, & will help you phenomenally. Know your emotions. There are only five basic ones. Everything you feel revolves around these five emotions. So, here is the key to uncover & unlock the door to your success & these emotions are... mad, sad, glad, afraid, & ashamed. EVERYTHING you feel revolves around one of these five emotions. Good luck in your journey."

"I do not fear the dark of night, the sadness of the day, or the tears that come my way. Rather, I take in the light, the happiness that comes my way, the love that satisfies, & blesses my every day."

July 20th

"When two people die & fly together just as a feather to above like a dove such as a kindred spirit, do you feel it?

"When you are engaging in conversation with someone, people may not care about you; they tend to care rather about themselves. Try to make it about them, & the conversation will flow more fluidly. If they want to know about you, they will let you know. Also, people may not care about the work you put into something; they seem to care more towards in a direction about your accomplishments."

July 22nd

"Love is many things. Let it roll the dice for you, not think twice for you, surprise you, & disguise you."

July 23rd

"Coal is like a true resting heart…it sits there for a while, for it is not lit. For a while, it rests. At one point, it was lit. It had a flame. It had a light. Now it rests…cold…unlit. It is only so long before it becomes lit again…when it does, it becomes life again. When it is lit, it is SO ALIVE! It is burning & full of life. But now it rests…waiting to be lit again."

"Being old is an idea, a state of mind. Only you control it. To me, you are not old until you are 80, 90, or even 100! You can be forever youthful for life, bittersweet, bitter, or an old soul...whatever the mentality you choose, I believe how you feel is how old you can be. Grant it: physically, your body will wear & tear, but happiness will sail your ship in an immense way & further than you can imagine. With this tool, you can quite possibly outlive others because the key to living longer than others is happiness. Just be happy, & these are words of a 92-year-old lady."

"Hope is one of the most powerful entities this Earth, life, & universe has to offer or provide. Hope is something that is not lost. One just chooses to lose it. It is a choice. It is magnified throughout this world. It is the only thing more powerful than fear besides love. It is shown through love, medicine, faith, people, families, friends, scary situations, & unknown situations. Faith & belief are hope's angels in arms. If you are unfamiliar with these three, then you are lost in life & need to find them. Without these, you are upriver without a paddle. Then where is your hope, faith, & belief?"

July 26th

"Life is a musical mosaic of a dance floor. It is filled with beautiful people to listen to, see, & move to. See them on the inside as a whole, listen to them with your heart like a drum, & dance your soul out with them."

July 27th

"The broken path is a path to be taken in this life because it is randomness that leads us to surprises & leaves us grateful in the end; after all, this life is about risk. When you get to Heaven, take the narrow path to the side gate. Everyone is fighting to get in the front, so why fight the fight, & just take the easy road? I think there will be a side road that leads to a side gate."

"To spiritually marry outside your vector is a risk worth taking so long as the chemistry is connected in a size that surpasses all circumstances & is foregone to the point of a power that makes sense to only the hearts of the ones that relate to clarity. Also, it is without a care of who is judging them form outward voices, echoes, & they fully understand each other through their hearts as well as souls on a higher level from deeper within."

"Listen to the music of life that beats just like the beat of your heart. As you dance through the avenues of a savior-faire-driven way, you march like the beat of a drum that passionately tells you which direction to go. Without any faux pas, you mind your manners spiritually & tell people that you will show respect as well as give them a reason why you are here because you have direction, & that is providence."

"I have heard you dance as though no one is watching you, love as though you have never been hurt before, sing as though no one can hear you, work like you do not need the money, & live as though heaven is on earth." This was by Alfred D. Souza." Well, I say... "write like it is your last page, laugh your loudest as if you are in your best company until your belly hurts & your face is red, dream like you are young, hope as if it were your last breath, believe in yourself like your best companion or lover. Enjoy yourself & this life like your favorite dessert, travel to new places, & try new foods because the surprise is the beauty of it, & party like there is no tomorrow."

July 31st

"A person's actions play an effect on what causes them to do or not do something. Cause & effect is common ground for results that have negative or positive results. Your feedback generates how you come back stronger or weaker. Growing from your mistakes makes you stronger. When you see your mistakes, you become stronger, you throw away your weaknesses, you build on yourself by growing positively, & that is an action caused by great motivation that can produce nothing but outstanding results. Through this challenging work & effort that you have wanted to produce, you should always be proud, & reward yourself abundantly for because you deserve every bit of success that you have achieved through your determination, devotion, dedication, strong will, effort, & endurance."

AUGUST

<h1 style="text-align:center">August 1st</h1>

"The pessimist looks at the road & says, 'That is too long. Forget this! I am turning back. It is pointless.' The optimist looks at the road with hope & says, 'That it is a beautiful journey. It will be an amazing trip! I cannot wait!' The realist looks at the road & says that you need to prepare by bringing food, water, and supplies, & you do not know what the weather will be. It is going to take you a long time to complete this road."

August 2nd

"One of the biggest problems I have noticed with people is that they do not want to be held accountable for their actions. Do yourself a favor, self-evaluate yourself in an effort of self-improvement. Do not be stubborn, blind, & act like there is nothing wrong with you as if you have no imperfections. Ask yourself this, is what I am doing at this point in my life right? Can I grow? Can I be a better person? Are there weaknesses I have that I can make stronger? Do others see weaknesses in me that I do not? If so, make these better. If & when you do, you will see & say that I have lived, learned, & grown since then! Then, that feeling that you will get will be a breath of fresh air because now your weaknesses are your strengths!!!"

August 3rd

"Devotion is an earnest attachment to a cause or person. So why not devote yourself to a person when you know in your heart it is right? Some people only come into your life once in a lifetime, heck once in a millennium! When this person comes, be brave & hold nothing back because chances are the beauty that has been waiting for the both of you will blossom like the miracle it is supposed to be. It is a gift to be devoted truly. Do not hold back & give your all because love, true love that is, truly is a wonderful, graceful, & miraculous thing."

August 4th

"Music as well as life are like life & love. You can live to love or live to love where music is living & loving throughout this life, & life is but a song & dance."

August 5th

"When times come that bring you down, falter not. Get up. Rejoice that you are still breathing & have life in your wings of flight. Find strength in your wings & fly. Search for wisdom & create outlets to consume your time that is creating your clutter. Do not conflict yourself with constriction. This life is your opening, so become that space that it can fill & occupy it with dedication, devotion, & enthusiasm."

August 6th

"When someone wants the best for you, pay attention to this. In fact, marvel at the ones who can simply just smile by saying nothing in a café. These people are special souls. We ignore the ones who want us, & the ones who want us- ignore us, but when you find the ones that want each other…hold tight & never let go. These souls make us happy just by being around one another because we understand each other so easily, & it makes life worth all the while."

August 7th

"When looking at something, a problem or situation, try not to look at it in a straight line- rather every angle. For example, imagine being in a stadium, standing high in the stands outside a row. Now look to your left, to your right, behind you, above you, down below you, way across from you, & all around you. There is a huge amount of space around you in that stadium. It is huge. Even when you look at a person, your first instinct should be what is it "inside" that person that makes that person who they are rather than what you first see? An approach can change everything you see in an instant. All problems & situations should be approached like a sphere rather than just a straight line. An open mind will always have an advantage over a closed one because it sees so much more. It knows more because it has the ability of wisdom, intuition, & insight."

"A dramatic impact is what is needed on someone to make others see the clarity of what truly exists. What is right & what is wrong are issues of a larger scale, & an example must be shown to them to see this dramatic change."

August 9th

"It amazes me how in the music industry of America ignorance sells & excels- then again, it does not. Moral of the story...if it feels good go for it. If it does not, then do not do it. Always follow your heart, for it will never lead you astray, not in your life, not in your relationships, not in your choices, not in your dreams, & not even on your wayward path. Just always follow the "music" of your life, sing happily, dance joyously, beat the drums of your heart out happily with constant laughter, & the notes will always without a doubt...play out just fine."

"Mark Twain said, "the two most important days of your life are the day you were born & the day you find out why." For me though, it is within the days of love; the day you find love, & the reason of why you are loved… because when you find love & the reason of being loved nothing else matters in this life. The one you are with & everything else seems to dissipate & just go away comfortably, soothingly, & that my friends are an even more powerful & thematic feeling than ever before. It is so captivating that you want to hold on to it tightly & never let it go."

August 11th

"Anyone can hurt you, bring you down, or even try to destroy you... but no one can ever take away all the beauty that you possess, contain, & will always have!!!"

"Happiness is an especially imperative & vital part of life. If you are not happy, then ask a friend or God, say, "Why am I not happy?" Seek it. Now… fight everything else until you have it all inside you because it is the best medicine that heals. It saves you. To me, you are in trouble if you are not happy."

"A bad spirit is one that wants to destroy, do harm, some detriment, or even evil. A good spirit is contagious, something to be valued, always maintained, & someone who will forever remain in your soul. Listen & listen intuitively... a "kindred spirit." Well, these are the ones "not" to go unnoticed. I tell you because a "kindred spirit" are the ones that when you cross paths with, you hold close to your heart, never let go of, always listen to with your heart, & not your mind. When you come across this type of spirit, escape with them wonderfully because nothing else will matter at all. Nothing good or bad will affect you because all you need will be right in front of you."

August 14th

"Belief is like holding onto something so tightly that you cannot let go of it, & it is wrapped so tightly around you that you have to just go with it. It drives you to the point where you just aim & go. You do not know why you are doing what you are doing, but you do it with 100% confidence. Something tells you whatever you are doing is right, & it is just that much right & that much worth it."

August 15th

"Faith is knowing that no matter what happens, good or bad, the outcome is going to work out for you because deep down in your gut-wrenched heart & soul, you know beyond a shadow of a doubt in your mind that whoever is in your life will be there for you because they care about you, that much, & God has put them in your life for an important & significant reason. You need not question it one bit because faith has become fate."

"If I am ever down, I just think of the people in my life that have made an impact on me... their beautiful & wonderful memories. Then, I can do nothing but smile & laugh. It is then that I am down no more but happy once more & laughter is once again, as always, the best, as easily produced, the best known & worldwide medicine."

"When searching for an answer, look within your heart & God will always show you a way through signs & symbolism by using your third eye. He shows you these things through literal signs, like street signs, words, things in movies, people's random conversations, people's names, music, dreams, & people that come into your life. Sometimes, the signs that he shows you are signs that are not meant for you but the ones that are. You will know because it will hit you in a way that makes you feel great in a strange way instead of a strange way that feels weird. The great ones are why He is so immaculately formidable!!!"

"No matter what comes in & out of your life, you must see the beauty of it. Wisdom is being able to discern the difference between good & bad. There are balances in the forces of nature in life. Call it what you will – karma, yin, yang, fate, the Word of God – we are all here to coexist. That is beauty enough that we are all here together living. Good or bad, the bad does not matter. Just to live is a gift. That is the greater good. If you can see life in each other & know that we are all here for a purpose then just love your life & love one another because ten years from now whatever hatred you had for one person, chances are it will not even matter. So, see the beauty of life in the amazing way that each person is. We are all beautiful in a subliminal way. You just must have the right heart of insight & know how to characterize it for the ones that really stand out."

"Knowledge is power indeed, but why try to understand everything? Some things we misunderstand. To seek knowledge is to know the unknown. When we understand misunderstandings, then clarity becomes so surreal to the point where excitement meets happiness & satisfaction. Bless the forever unknown because soon enough we will understand, & that is a glorious gift to the ones who get to know the unknown & understand what is misunderstood."

"Trust is a choice, not something given & it is something that is built. Respect is earned, not just given. Knowing someone or something takes time, just like anything else. Love is something that is felt, not just an idea. The steps of loving someone involve trust, respect, knowing, & then there is love. One of the biggest problems in America is trust. If you meet the right person, trust is an extremely easy opportunity so long as they are true. There are more good people in this world than bad. I guarantee it & genuinely believe it. For if there was not, we would prevail very easily, & the goodness in this world would cease to exist. Be thankful for all the good, & evil will not know what hit it in its ugly face."

August 21st

"When you find yourself lost in this life, ask yourself these 3 basic questions: 1) Do I truly know myself? 2) What have I done to get where I am now? & 3) What can I do in my life to better myself healthily, every day? Not just physically but emotionally, mentally, & spiritually, how can I make my life better in 'these ways?' Happiness is a choice, not a demand."

"A rich heart is the road to inner success while poverty-stricken hearts (the hearts that lie, cheat, deceive, conspire, steal, instigate, hurt, & antagonize) are the ones that will forever be poor at heart. Only change, because there is always change, will prove who is rich in this life & who is poor in life. Philosophically, money means nothing. It is just paper that controls too much. People's hearts make this world go around, not money. It is why passion, compassion, hope, faith, honesty, humbleness, selflessness, & love survive."

August 23rd

"It is amazing in life how the moments in life that you share with the ones you love bring you closer to one another."

"Talent… what a wasted gift. I heard from the movie Titanic by Leonardo DiCaprio, 'Life is a gift, & I do not intend on wasting it.' All the time, people say, 'I cannot do that anymore,' 'I wish I would have done that more,' or 'If I could go back, I would have done this & that.' If you have talent, are exceptionally good at something, or are the absolute best at something, do not hide that from the world or yourself. Talent is one of the most wasted commodities of what life offers as a gift. You must show the world who you are & not hide it. I have said before, too, that 'the heart is bright. You are the only one who can keep it from going dim.' So, here we are… now. It is never too late to display your gifts, no matter what age you are. Do what you know is best for yourself. It is ok to be selfish sometimes if it is for the right purpose & benefits you abundantly. Let life make you shine by using what you are best at. Do not wait any longer. Now is the time; the best part of your life is right now. So, show off some."

"Life is about sacrifice. You get this life once, not twice. When you give up what you have, what are you left with? Are you left with nothing or everything? Many people do not know how to think for themselves when everything is gone. What will you do when no one is around? Sacrifice your time, your job, your money, or your relationships, & you will see how humble life can really be. For it is in giving that we receive, & God as well as life will show you a funny sense of humor."

August 26th

"Learning is not just about what you get taught. It is about taking what you already know & making something constructive out of it. You are always a student in this life, for even the teacher can learn from the student no matter how much the teacher thinks they can teach. As humans, we are always students of this wonderful puzzle we call life."

August 27th

"Ask yourself this, 'Do I work for survival or passion?' If you work to survive, then you are a cliché' like every other American working the average paycheck to paycheck, wondering why you are doing what you are doing on a day-to-day basis that leads nowhere. However, if you work for & with passion & compassion, then that is what will separate you widely from the pack, & you will go so much further in life. You will never have to wonder anything about why it is you are doing what you are doing because passion holds no boundaries & is limitless, whereas no passion leads to questioning as to why am I doing what I am doing."

"This life can be as big as you ever wanted it to be, or it can be as tiny as your own little city. Dreams are what make us, shape us, & guide us for things as big as the passion & desire that never tires of the stars that light our path for the wayward journey of our ways of the days & nights that never seem to stay."

"I can see the night stars that hang & comfort the peaceful night sky. They tell the moon that everything is ok. Because even from miles unheard of away, they know that the best will shine. I can see the moon glowing, giving us the dreams we have always wanted. The night is the peace that wants the day to be the same. Glow on, with every inch of your soul that burns & then releases fire as well as a desire because like the moon & stars, oh how bright you so effortlessly shine."

"It is so powerful that an idea, a dream, a goal, love, happiness, prayer, focus, meditation, hope, faith, belief, & God, together can make you anything you ever want to be as a directed, guided, & purposeful individual in this lifetime."

"Every good story has a great, even the best of endings. Sure, there is tragedy, heartache, pain, & strife, but it all mends in the end & shows us that every good thing worth talking about, seeing, doing, & living is worth it in the end & making memories about. Yes, a delightful story has the greatest of endings, as does this conviction we call... life."

SEPTEMBER

September 1st

"An artist's art with heart is never parted nor departed. A musical composer's composure of composition is never frozen.

A dancer's dance is never danced deadly, but rather steadily & readily because of spirit & soul- they feel it whole. A writer's work is never written smitten & it is never finished nor diminished. It cannot bend to an end because, like cancer, it needs a constant answer. Finally, timely, the love for all of these never ceases, like the rotation of the Earth on its axis, so is the flotation of art that is… art, the beautiful. Stay, never astray. Just obey as light does foresight the dawning of the yawning of the sincere, adhere day. Yay."

"This life is meant for certainty & clarity. Why waste the truth that is meant to be? For all humanity, let knowledge be power. Seek truth, but know, yes, know that wisdom will always prevail. Shackles bind you to the unknown, but freedom of the righteous & truth with wisdom will always free your mind & calm your soul. Having a vision, insight, intuition, an open mind, heart, & a clear conscience are the necessities & tools that will lead & guide you. Having a clear outlook on what you seek to be answered in this mysterious, glorious, & wonderful journey of life."

September 3rd

"We are bound to this world by wanting to know truth… truth of things, all things, & even things from the past. Why? It only conflicts with you. If we do not know it, we will find it. If we cannot find it, we will seek it. If we cannot seek it, we will wait, & it will find us because somehow, someway, whatever we are meant to know, we will know, & whatever we do not will not matter. Knowledge is power, indeed, but people, you will learn that some things in this life are supposed to be left misunderstood, unsaid, & lived in the present. It is better that way for the better good of humanity purposely. So, learn to let things go, leave things unsaid, live in the present, & life will be so much easier."

September 4th

"It does not matter how much you know your emotional content or try to control it; your emotions will always happen & come upon you like the weather. The rain, lightning, thunder, & sunny days will always happen naturally. Even if you know yourself & try to control yourself, you cannot weather the storm. With God, prayer, thanks for living, family, friends, love, hope, & faith, any emotional content will be cleared just like blue skies peacefully to right where you began as if the weather was clear all along."

September 5th

"People can have the brightest of spirits
Yet the loneliest of hearts.
People see this, become afraid, & fear this.
When true love finds you, it never departs."

"Like a feather, I had to fly away to a brand-new day. Today, I breathe such clean, comfortable air... but oh, how I do & must care that sometimes your words on my lips are a memory that still exists. Tomorrow, I may wake up & not even think about you, but you are never forgotten, not now, not today, not even then. I go on happily, always remembering my love, my best friend. You are never a shadow that allows me to strike evil, but rather an angelic light that shines a wayward path for me of true enlightenment, for you taught me great & beautiful things that I will forever carry with me. Although days of rain have come & nights of pain, I just think of your amazing smile from time to time & the laughter we shared because I know that true happiness & love, like you, are out there. For that, I am forever grateful & thankful."

September 7th

"If one can learn to live in the present, that is why it is called a 'gift,' they will never have a problem living. The breath that we are breathing right now is ALL that matters! The what-ifs do not matter. What is to come, what might happen, & what has happened does not matter. If one can learn to live in the moment, then life is as easy as breathing as life IS a series of moments!!!"

"I do not have the type of person I prefer. However, if I am a type, of whatever classification I am, then I am the best type of whatever type that type is to the utmost exponential result."

September 9th

"My mind is like a stadium... it constantly needs great &
even sometimes, yes, spectacular performances."

"Patience is like empathy... it cannot be taught – you either have it, or you do not. If you want to be taught these entities, then you have to teach yourself, & it takes time just like anything else that can be taught."

9/11 REFLECTION

9/11 September 11th

"Years ago today, we never saw it coming… the planes flying so hard, so fast & humming. Now, it is today – a brand-new day. For everyone who died on 9/11, we pray. May they rest in peace, God bless their souls, & to all who tried & died to rescue women as well as men… may God bless them too. Amen."

"In this life, I hope you find whatever it is that you are looking for… & whatever is looking for you finds you the same."

September 13th

"L.I.F.E.- Let It Fail You Easily or Live by Inspiration Fully Every Day. The choice is yours, every day."

September 14th

"Dying in this life is you choosing how you want to live this life right here, right now, here on out fully."

"Giving never goes unnoticed & is rewarded one way or another… but TAKING intentionally always gets punished one way or another. It is a king's rule."

September 16th

"A word is a word because it means something… anything, but it means nothing until you 'feel it.'

"Absolution rule: Never say never, say ever. Then try not saying ever; say forever. Then do not say forever; say moreover. Then say furthermore. Then say moreover again & again & again always. Then realize there are always 'ways' to do 'more' things over & over again, never ever the same forever the further you go in life, more times over & over & over again. Then, say 'over.' Afterward, you come to know that nothing is ever over, & you are at peace once & for all."

September 18th

"You do not have to count on music. You do not even have to know it. You just must 'feel' it. It sometimes becomes a joke; it sometimes becomes something real; it sometimes becomes life. It really is the story of life, & oh, music… I love how you move my soul through this journey of life. You will never stop evoking me & invoking me in the most irrevocable of manners. Oh, you lovely music, you… how I so love thee in the upmost promissory of manners."

"If you want to blame anybody for anything, then blame yourself."

"Having too much pride or arrogance is the road to overconfidence & cockiness. Strive to be humble, kind, & sincere, for that is what people will adhere to."

"There is no such thing as a foolish question, just a fool who will not ask the question because you will never get your answer to an unanswered question."

"It is in lying that people give a false lie in which they will deny, & it is in giving that lie that they will live that lie. Lying is like dying on the inside, while dying on the outside is always trying. The lie will make them want to deny, but if you know how to give yourself truly, you can live your life purely & of course, beautifully. Consequently, it is in living that we die comfortably, & it is in dying that we live to lie forever in the Heavens & in peace where an eternal high of bliss will never cease. Living & dealing with an angel could never be a lie."

"Life is a poem. Read it & understand its many beautiful metaphors."

"It is in apologizing & letting go of your pride that you sometimes find an apology in someone else. Even if it is to have that peace & forgiveness, it is worth that peace. It is worth peace of mind, & forgiveness. For it is better to have peace & love in your heart to always rid yourself of hatred. Hatred is a poisonous piece of clothing to wear, & it needs to be taken off to breathe freely as well as spiritually."

"If you want to make someone happy, then simply know what makes them happy, point blank. If you want to make yourself happy, ask someone who knows you to do something to make you happy. If your life is boring, do something about it. If your love life has lost its spark, then think about how that spark got lit in the first place. If there are things you want to do, then do them. If your job sucks, leave it. If your food tastes bad, then tell someone, & do not eat it. If you are bored, get off your lazy self & get out in the world. Make moments like taking pictures, singing in the car, or playing pranks on someone. Dance, take walks on sunny days, & try foods you have never had before. Go & see places you have never seen before. Get in touch with that old friend you have not talked to seen or heard from in forever. Play with kids & animals or see a movie, write a letter to a family member, something, anything. Talk to an elderly person. If you keep having bad dreams, then surround yourself with happiness, laughter, & love. Do whatever you can to find a way to laugh until you cry, or your face falls off & your cheeks hurt from laughing so hard & your belly hurts so much you must pee… because there is no greater thing than true happiness."

"If you are going to do something, do something right. If you are going to fight, fight the good fight. If you are going to see something, see the light. If you are going to live… then live with ALL your might."

"Some people say I would not wish death upon anyone... but what about the circumstances when someone is suffering & in pain? I say rest ashore. Peace be with you. I wish you a peaceful journey as you sail your waters to the skies of the Heavens to... not death. I wish you life ever after. So, I wish life to anyone who deserves it. Would you not want a better life? Everyone wants a beautiful afterlife. So, when in pain & you have done all that you can do on this lovely Earth, sail the winds of freedom. On eagle's wings soar to the doves in the sky of peace to Heaven's arms. Let them embrace you eternally, peacefully, in a lovely way, & beautifully. Believe in life, for it is in dying that we forever live."

September 28th

"Anger turns to violence, which turns to silence. The mix of the water with light in your world turns dark. Happiness turns to less. She or he comes into your world playing you like strings on a violin as if you are her or his concert. This is a lesson learned. Keep on dancing. Keep on singing. Do not look back. Stay on track. Do not get caught up in the mix. There will be no remix. The road is long. Keep singing your song. Know where your heart belongs. Be fun like the sun. To sadness, chew it up, for you are done. Sing, give praise & glory to the Heavens as well as the sun. You have only just begun. To love… you will never ever give up."

"Self-discovery is a creation of one's inner self. You are already created to be what you already are. It is in self-definition in which you recognize your inner strengths & blossom them like petals from a flower. Growing in life never stops like a bee constantly at work; sweet is the life of self-discovery."

"Learn to see the light & beauty in life through your difficulties. Otherwise, darkness will cloud your judgment & ugliness will be all you see very easily."

OCTOBER

October 1st

"Fairytales & love stories are not just a fictional database of an encyclopedia with pros & cons. There are only good endings if & when done right with the right faith – belief, too, that is followed with hope & love accompanied by truth. The essence of volunteering a miracle of blessings from above excludes the works of fear, anger, evil, destruction, vile, & hatred. Fairytales are a 'reality' that idealists will never understand because love is a crown that rules over any kingdom. So, it is worshiped only by the ones who are true believers, & true believers do not need proof that the idealist needs because, for them, hope, belief, faith, & love just exists to them easily."

October 2nd

"This life is not just stirring, echoes, whispers, or winds that come in the days & nights with meaningless voices without thoughts & interpretations. There are points of recognition, signs, & symbolism everywhere that have crashes, cymbals, drums, bangs, & loud signals. The problem is that communication is broken. One of the biggest problems today is that echoes of thoughts in people's minds do not make it to their voices. People do not speak their minds openly enough & communication is a fault commonly not expressed enough as it should be today. It is a lost art. Revive, learn, & practice daily this lost art because it is essential to living & loving."

"There is only one way to live, & that is up. In other words, you must live it up. Every day. All day. Your whole life. Live it up. Give it up. To God. Live it all up. Just live it up. Always."

"One of the keys to happiness for this life is loving life, being thankful for what you have, & making anything out of everything… that is nothing."

"Sometimes what we WANT in life is not what we NEED, & what we need in life is not what we want. Sometimes in life, a CHANCE will pass us by, & a chance may not come again. Sometimes in life, a CHOICE is presented in front of you, & that choice is that chance. Sometimes, a CHANGE will come in which we may or may not make that change, & to change, we have to make that choice. Sometimes, we "want" & "need" this "chance" to make this "choice," & we choose this choice to "change." But sometimes we need not change at all because we have all that we ever wanted or needed."

October 6th

"Strength is one's guidance in life, knowing that no matter how hard the winds may be pushing against you in your sea of life, no storm can ever push you off your ship because you are the captain of your ship. Your spirit is incredibly too powerful & mighty for you to ever think of sinking, swimming, or drowning. So, guide yourself with the wind of strength. Refuse the storm, & free your spirit from sorrows."

October 7th

"Life is not about knowing what to do & what not to do. It is about knowing when to do something, where to do something, who you are doing something with, & why you are doing something with that person at that time."

October 8th

"Life is about living happiness. So, if we are not smiling or laughing, then why are we living? Get busy dying or get busy living."

October 9th

The Winner's Blessing

"May your life beat like a drum, your heart never become numb, your friends remain near, & blue skies stay clear.

May your spirit dance like the rain, your family feel no pain, you spread your wings as you soar through the air & show your enemies care.

May you have enjoyable conversation while showing appreciation, between you & me... respect the elderly. Smile all the while, find love above, & dare not to be scared.

May your shadows become a glimmer, the winds never be a whisper, the tides make you a swimmer, & the faintest of echoes shout within you, crash like cymbals, & make you a... winner."

"If you can look inside yourself one day & see absolutely nothing wrong… then you know you are doing something wrong. If you can start every day fresh with a clean slate and see everything inside yourself at that moment at the start of every day… then there is nothing that can go wrong. Henceforth, as you see the good inside yourself… thank God for creating every brand-new day."

October 11th

"To love or not to love – that is the question."

October 12th

"I do not wish to be everything to everyone, but I would like to be something to someone."

"Passion is what fuels a soul for desire. It makes it an eternal blue flame of fire kindled by a kindred spirit. It then connects it to a web of an infectious & electric touch. Only the starlit eyes of a lightning & thunderous heart can tell this through an earthquake that quakes of love, passion, & a fury fire of love. Feeling pounded within the depths, cavities, crevices, & craters of the moonlit heart & soul… one can truly feel the passion."

October 14th

"Happiness is the key to the survival of life, yet joy is eternal. Happiness leads to tenacity & resiliency. It is then the avenue that leads to the road of anywhere you would ever desire to go freely without any chains that have ever held you down before."

"Adventure is a curiosity that "raised" the cat."

October 16th

"You cannot use the past to predict the future or think about the what-ifs in life even though the what-ifs involve logic. Thinking about the what-ifs involves the future, anxiety, & nervousness. Rather, swim in the present & you will find that your dreams are right there at your fingertips in front of your face. All you must do is touch them today. So, reach out & make something of it now… for the time is now."

"Unforgiveness is a poisonous pill once swallowed. Chew it up & spit it out. Forgive. Forgive because pride… bad pride is just as poisonous as a pill that you should never swallow."

October 18th

"The definition of best friends is two people who, when reconnecting, can just pick right back up where they left off when they last saw each other. It still seems as if not much has changed at all between them because they know each other that much, that well."

October 19th

"A person with a humble heart will have a home welcoming them with an open door. A person without a humble heart will have a door slammed in their face."

"Life should be like wing chun kung fu... simple, direct, & no wasted time redirecting you in any way possible with an effective outcome."

"I believe that music is a beautiful, gorgeous, amazing, & impressive gift that transcends from the Earth to the Heavens. If it is not or does not, then it did a long time ago. It existed in a world extremely far away. It has a curious, mesmerizing, & peculiar connection that is truly relatable & magical. What a blessing & beautiful gift music wonderfully is."

"An art, or art itself, is something that has no limitations, limits, or blockades. It is bound by infinite expression to be told, is understood openly, & freely to expand the mind in a creative manner."

"Your 5 core feelings are: Mad, Sad, Glad, Afraid, & Ashamed. EVERYTHING you feel revolves around these five core feelings.

Anger: it is an enemy. You cannot let your enemy control you. Divide it. Stand AGAINST it! Find the strength & calm it to a restful peace.

Sadness: it is your crutch. It is up to you to lean on it or get up off that crutch. If you do not get up, then you will drown in sorrow. It wants to bring you down so DO NOT let it!!!

Gladness: it is your best friend. Do not lose it. Find it at all costs. It is UNBELIEVABLY valuable, & once you have it… try hard not to let it go.

Fear: it is your dark ally. Conquer it & your worst fears can be your best friends.

Shame: it is your poison. If you let guilt grab hold of you, then fight it, defend against it, & know it. When you understand it, it can NOT hold you down, & it will flee from you! Otherwise, it will be a complete sickness.

& Love: it is a mystery. Seek it or let it find you. Once you discover it, do NOT EVER let it go. Because love conquers & strengthens ALL these core feelings!!!

& Music: it may not be a core feeling, but it channels ALL these emotions! It heals & provides a safe harbor to cure all of these if you discover what that is like. If you are lost, then get lost in music & you will find your answers there."

October 24th

"Life is a canvas. Paint it. Make it colorful. Make it your own beauty. Make it wonderful. Life is a canvas."

STAR PRAYER

October 25th

"Though the stars in the sky brighten your view, they will always be there for you. Though the stars may come at night & fade by day, they will always be with you day by day. Though the stars may tend to glisten, your heart will forever shine & to them- listen. Though the stars may be bright, they are always there to show you the light. Though the stars may make you wonder who & what you are, they are always in the sky, & they are forever showing you a wayward path until the day you die. Keep shining little stars in the sky, for we know where you are but do not know why."

"You cannot change yourself or "re-create" yourself. You will always be you. If you 'think' it is for the good, then do it. But do not just hope… KNOW! If it is not right, then stop trying the fight, take what is good, & turn it into yourself."

"MUSIC FOR ME"

October 27th

"Music for me is sacred. It is an expression of love. For me, music is my health. Music is not just something that you listen to. It is something that you feel. You live it. You breathe it. You see it. You dance to it. It can be dark, light, or colorful. You emote it. It feeds all your emotions – anger, sorrow, happiness, fear, & even guilt. It helps me physically, emotionally, mentally, & spiritually. It is my medicine. It is my health. It comes in many shapes & sizes. It shapes you in uncontrollable ways. It is something that you dream about. It is an escape. It is an essential & important way of living for me. Most of all, it tells stories & is a journey that you can relate to for any given situation. It travels all throughout this world in many cultures, telling all kinds of stories, & it is felt globally & culturally in its own unique way. It gives me Goosebumps all the time, & I can never get enough of it – it is like an addictive drug. It is very inspirational. I love to sing it, dance to it, write it, play it, & I cannot get enough of it. I am in love with music. What can I say... we are artists."

"It is good to be different, to stand out because people do not like the norm; they get bored with it. They like abnormalities. Being different is not weird; it is just a different kind of normality that people should choose to understand & like more often because being different & weird is what makes life more fun, enjoyable, & worth living for."

October 29th

"Treat your money like you have no money."

"True love is life's pinnacle of a blessing, its most precious comfort, & the most rewarding satisfaction one could ever yearn for."

HALLOWEEN REFLECTION

October 31st

"God is your light, & love is your beacon. The devil is the ship he wants you to sail away on… rest ashore."

NOVEMBER

"Step back. Clear your head. Realize what is true, what has substance, & value. Let reality set back in, you will be back in your normal state, & you will find that breathing is as easy as walking."

November 2nd

"Do you know what smart is? Resourceful... meaning a smart person can use what is around them & make the best of any outcome or any given environment. They can also utilize it, & exponentially use it to their utmost potential."

"Determining the outcome of a situation rather than just letting nature take its course can possibly set you up for failure. For, if you worry too much about the result or the future instead of just living in the present moment, all can be lost, & life can just pass you by right in front of your face blindly."

THOUGHTS ON LIFE & LOVE

November 4th

"They say life is too short... I say it is transport. You live for a reason, as you die for a reason. You leave this earth with many things in your heart & mind. Yet what matters is what compiles your soul. What makes your soul... really?... God? Love? Strength? Determination? Indomitable Spirit? Self-Control? Patience? Devotion? Dedication? Will? Survival? Visions? Dreams? A catalyst for all of this? What makes your soul is your Maker. It is blank when born. After birth, you are meant to be glued to someone... yes, a "soulmate." Do you think you make your own soul? It is shaped throughout this life. Follow your heart always above your mind because the feelings from your heart always overpower the mind, outweigh the mind, & have a feeling unmatched & indescribable that the mind will 'never' have. So, feel in 'the heart' that there IS a soulmate out there for EVERY person on this planet. If they do not find it in a loved one, then they find it in a friend, a parent, a sibling, a grandparent, aunt, uncle, cousin, or even a stranger. If not these, then I believe death will grant you what you deserve. This life & love will live happily ever after as long as you live & know love. This life IS about love, among other things, yet love is real & all around us. I am sorry if love is not a part of someone's life, but once you find it… it is something you can never let go. For me, it is my soul mate. The love of my life. The angel that saved me from darkness & makes me a better man every day just by loving me. This love takes me to a place I have never been before. It is through her that love has shown me light. So, I challenge many to find love. Do not forsake this

327

God-given gift. Life & Love work hand in hand to transport you above to eternity. At least I see life as love & love as life, alive within a feeling wielded indescribable. Life is constant music in motion, moving to move you in a better direction with God's aid. I end this with listening to the music of life & love the tunes of life's journey, for it will make you dance your whole way to Heaven with the one you love. Whatever you love to do… keep your dreams & prayers alive as you dare to dream even bigger, love even larger, laugh even harder, & celebrate life's joys & gifts endlessly. Amen."

November 5th

"They say there are many races & many faces (I cannot remember who said this, but I heard it somewhere), but all in all, there is only one race, & that, my friends... is the human race."

"Learn from the days of sorrow… so that from them you can borrow to make the future a better tomorrow."

"Negativity is a vice & crutch for itself. Optimism is truly hidden from the opaqueness of negativity. There are more valuable things to come with great blessings through positivity... instead of being let down by uncertainty, disapproval, & a poor attitude. Stay positive, for it is a road to success that negativity will usually be envious of."

November 8th

"Life is a book. Well then, now, open it up & read it for all it is worth. For it is full of surprises and signs, & it will never stop entertaining you & guiding you. It will go on & on to new chapters of beginnings, endings, happiness, sadness, laughter, romance, heartfelt riches, & who knows what else you may find. Just open life's book & explore its wonderful gifts & riches bestowed from above like an opened treasure chest. Explore it with glimmer, wonder, & a young heart."

November 9th

"A life path is defined to me not by when you are born but by how & which directions you take in your journey of love directed above from God. This life is decided by your choices in what you choose, & in doing so, you decide your true destiny. Your heart controls a lot of it. Your soul is what guides your heart, and so is your faith. The steps that you take – little by little – become enchanted by the tapestry of the multitude of gentle hearts that touch you along the way. What you take with you along this 'path' is yours to choose. The one person that sticks with you, your 'soulmate,' THIS person is YOUR life 'partner.' Life is a gift intended not to be wasted, so journey it well. Live well. Laugh well. Love well. Fight for what you love. Make peace often. Challenge anger with smiles of joy. Pray for you & your life partner to reach the summit with a melody SO harmonious that a trumpet will have to blow SO hard just to be heard. A drum will have to beat SO hard & fast just to keep up with the rhythm & sound of your hearts because you two together are that insanely POWERFUL! & TOGETHER... y'all have created a partnered life path!!!"

"Never fight a fight that does not need fighting. Rather, find peace & maintain that peace."

"This life is full of possibilities. The only limitations are the ones you make. You make your own choices, & your choices set your possibilities. Live this life as a gift. Do not waste it. Limit yourself to no limits. Create possibilities that are possible. Set no limits on your possibilities. The mere fact that there are no limits & an exponential availability of possibilities is one of life's most precious gifts. You are your best weapon of choice in life's battles. Thank the future, for it is what you can create. Do not hold the past so tightly, for today is what matters most & live for today because it is living in the moments that define us. Fill your life with complete happiness, & once you have found that happiness…create from there."

November 12th

"Life should be like canoeing down a river... everything should be beautiful around you, & you should be at peace with everything around you. Yes, there may be rapids, and the waters may get rough, but there is nothing within these waters that you cannot manage by paddling through with God's grace. These are your waters of life, beauty, grace, & peace, blessed as well as cleansed by God with great appreciation. You should be thankful, soak in these waters, & enjoy the nurture of people & God's gifts that he has bestowed upon you every day. Notice the beauty that surrounds you endlessly throughout your lifetime. It does not matter what lies ahead of this river, so long as you know that you can paddle through what you are going through now. Fill yourself with peace, God's grace, His love, & the love of the ones around you."

"Time is timeless. Love is timeless. Love does not hold time accountable. Do not rush yourselves, for you will ruin yourselves. Never be in a hurry. There is nowhere to go but into the grasp of life & arms of love. Rushing, hurrying, & always trying to be somewhere as soon as possible will only conflict your mind. Rest. Rest your mind. Come to find peace & be at peace. Why do you hurry so much? Just find yourself in an outlet of love & peace. Love your surroundings & let it surround you with peace & comfort. Do not let it control you. You control it. It is your time. It is your love. It is your peace. For your love is in no rush, no hurry, no stress, & is timeless as so is life."

November 14th

"Sometimes what you think for yourself, others know better for you… meaning sometimes what you think is better for yourself, loved ones know what is better for you. You should listen to what they have to offer you to better yourself rather than being stubborn & fighting yourself. You are only hurting yourself by not listening to the ones who love you when they know what is best for you, & it will make your life much easier by just simply listening to them & giving them effort."

"If you think you used to have something within you, & it is lost & hidden, then know that all is not lost or buried within you. Rather, find it within you & rekindle all that is lost because it never went anywhere. It is in you all along the way in your walk of life. All you have to do is see the light, & light what has been dark."

"Set the fire in your hearts. Fuel the fire & ignite the flames. Feed the desire. Tear it apart. Never retire. Burn it. Never become a liar. Fly. Follow it. Swallow what is dark & scary. Are you not tired of being weak & weary? Achieve what is forgotten & not yet touched. Feel the love & chew away anger & such. Know yourself. Spit out selfishness & become selfless because you are never helpless. Your heart always knows this. Your mind retracts this & shows this, your soul whispers, & it echoes sweet winds of inspiration which blow this."

"Do what you do. However, whatever you do... 'care' about what you do."

"Knowing your own self-worth is predominantly more valuable than letting another value yourself."

"A goal is nothing but anything until it is truly conquered on the inside, then outwardly achieved on the outside by an action."

November 20th

"To deny one's right to pray is to deny one's right to live."

November 21st

"Sometimes things happen that we have no control over. Do we let it control us? Or do we try to control it? One thing is constant... a force to be reckoned with... love. It breaks barriers beyond means universally unimaginable. When anything happens that we do not understand, all we can do is love, comfort, & rather than try to understand these things... just love. Love the ones around you. Know that whether things happen for a reason or not, know that love, passion, compassion, affection, strength, courage, wisdom, peace, endurance, comfort, laughter, & the ones closest to you will always happen to you in the best way possible. If ANYTHING happens or tries to control you – let THESE 12 things control you."

"Be a leader, not a follower, but if you are going to be a leader, then be a really good one. Know your strengths. Know your weaknesses. You will fall but never fail. If you think you failed, then rise. Stand tall. Know that tomorrow is ALWAYS a new day. Start EVERY day fresh & clean. Remember that yesterday mended today. Terrible things fall apart so that wonderful things can come together. Good things take time, but wonderful things happen all at once. The storm will always pass. Others may stare at you, but they can never take what you have. You are the strongest out there that you can quite possibly be. With God by your side & love, you can conquer ANYTHING that tries to stand in your way. You are your worst fear. If you conquer your inner worst fears, then you can achieve whatever you want. It is not hard. You just make it hard. The only unique forces that are stronger than fear are love & hope. If you believe this, you can conquer any fear. Know this. Believe this. Just know that this life is yours to take & soar. Now, fly away. Just spread your wings, look up, breathe, and say to yourself, "OK, God, I got this." Believe in yourself, release, & just go."

"Where are the minds that are kind? Where are the genuine people who have generosity? Where are the real that have reality? Where are the hearts that are heart-felt, & the likeable that are like-minded? Because we want a kind mind, genuine, generous, real heart, & like-minded person."

"Pray for good. Hope for the best. Never expect the worst. Change what is bad & be determined for strength, passion, focus, & love."

"Living in the moment is many things: confidence, clear vision, being fearless, having love, courage, strength, wisdom, experience, being happy, comfort, security, & a good spirit. Mind your heart. It is in moving the moment in which beautiful things happen. Take all the above with you for your journey ahead. Pausing & celebrating it now, dividing all behind you, looking up, & breathing out will suffice for you. Faith, hope, love, happiness, & God will truly bless you. With this, you simply just could & quite possibly... own, love, & be thankful for EVERY living moment!!!"

THE "PRESENT": "Live in the present, for tomorrow opens up presents & brings a positive presence. That is why you take from yesterday & make tomorrow a gift today... a present, make today your presence, & present yourself with what you have learned from yesterday. So, make today your gift by living in the present TODAY presently... a gift every day. For 'the present' is a gift & where true happiness & the happiest of people live."

TRUE LOVE SHORT POEM

November 27th

"True love does not come by looking for Love.

It comes by looking for you from above.

Patience is a virtue. Faith is, too.

Believing in the two is a love true for two.

That is why it takes 'two' to have this belief, & through this belief with patience, hope, faith, & love so true is why love is so true.

Love WILL find both of YOU!!

Just believe in love, which is all you two must do.

Just know that there IS someONE out there for BOTH of YOU!!!

& It will be because of this why you say I LOVE YOU!!!

& It IS because of this why you will live happily ever after

& Say forever, 'Yes Baby, I LOVE YOU; I DO, & I WILL ALWAYS & FOREVER TRULY LOVE YOU TRUE!!!'"

November 28th

"Life without aim is like an artist's brush without paint. With the right direction, you can complete the picture & create an amazing… beautiful painted life."

November 29th

"The gift of giving is a life's worth full of living."

353

November 30th

"Why does everything happen so fast?

Can the past stay the past?

Can something be looked past?

Why do so many questions have to be asked?

Something should just be believed & relieved.

Everything happens for a reason.

Why does treason have to have a heathen?

Why do women make it a point to understand men?

We do not understand women. Amen.

Understanding something is just accepting, not questioning.

Answers are not supposed to be answered.

They are supposed to be 'lived' & 'journeyed.'

Get down on your knees & pray to the sky.

Do not ever question why. Live for today & think about the day you are going to die.

Do not ever look back. You will find yourself sitting on a tac.

It will hurt & give pain. There will be no gain.

It is not easy to forget, but, it is so extremely easy to just love.

Live. Love. Celebrate life, & love. These are answers to life."

DECEMBER

December 1st

"When love finds you... a journey does not just begin. It leaves. It soars away to a cloud, shares its deepest treasures of the heart, & takes you on a flight to a deserted island where only the eye of the beholder knows where the real hidden treasures lie in these buried sands. For ONLY a soul mate understands the hidden treasures of this eternal voyage that is of a married vacation of a splendid, blended heart."

December 2nd

"With hope, belief, faith, believing in yourself, loving yourself, loving others fully, & letting others do the same to you... is how you could hold the key to your own victory."

"God is Good. God is great! Thank you, God, for this impressive ride of a life-love date! It is a date that lasts a whole life, & a love that is that of a wife. It has always been, for her, a husband. It is a kind of love that is that of a lifetime, & a love that is once in a lifetime. So, thank you, God, on this day for a love life date… a love that is a love that is like a date. It is full of happiness & love from above. My whole life to you, I thank & give praise to You. For that special one full of fun, to you every day I pray & thank you for her or him on this day."

"Life is full of surprises. God works in mysterious ways. Your life can be gone in an instant. It is because of this that you can never take life for granted. You can lose everything you love in the blink of an eye. When you wake up every day… you put your pants on each leg, knowing what you have each day. But what you do not know is what could happen for the rest of the day. God is funny. He always smiles at you without knowing. You do not even know what it means until you realize the path that he is pointing at you. Always use your third eye. You must be big on signs & symbolism. At least I am. All I know is what I have, & that is my heart. I will always follow it more than my head. If I do that, then I can never go wrong. It is because of this that I know that God will always show me the way with the ones I love & make my life so miraculously special. Just remember your day may not come tomorrow. NEVER take life or anyone or anything for granted, keep the ones that you love remarkably close at heart, & always listen to what God tells you in your heart."

"Find God in your hearts today, I pray, because tomorrow may never come. What may come tomorrow is His Kingdom."

"Food is like your best friend... you cannot live without it, there are some things you like about it, some things you do not, & it will ALWAYS be there for you."

"Life is about taking risks with dedication. You will never know how much life is out there until you take that chance- that opportunity... seize it, grasp it, develop it, cultivate it, captivate it, & apply devotion from yourself inwardly, outwardly, from the heart & spirit... truly. Never letting go of this will show you how much a chance is worth because it will, without fail, leave you absolutely grateful in the end if & when you do it right."

December 8th

"Life is about experiences, journeys of love with the ones you have loved, strength, & surviving these trials & tribulations with love. Because of this, life portrays your heart with experiences that you have given to others of your strife & courage about these stories of the ones you have loved that are most cherished, closest, dearest, & sacred to your heart."

"If you leave a long-lasting impression, chances are… you may not leave any depression."

ONE PERFECT KISS

December 10th

"A Kiss is Heaven sent – a miracle in an Angelic disguise & is only what YOU yourself can make of it. Be yourself. Be true. Be bold. Be brave. Dare to take this chance... but take your time. Do not rush & be sure you get it right the first time because you may NEVER get this chance again! So, make it magical like the Fourth of July Fireworks, a blazing bonfire on a beach on a great calm summer's starlit night sky, & rare shooting stars that you see in her eyes for the very first time. As you do it, go with the flow & leave that special woman of your dreams wanting you more & more & NEVER wanting to let you go out of her sight. For it is an amazing, phenomenal, magical, out of this world, Heavenly, memorable, unforgettable, & most of all, THEE "One Perfect Kiss" that SHE herself will NEVER forget!!!"

DO NOT TRY…JUST FLY:

December 11th

Fixing someone is like trying to put a square into a "TRY-angle." That person is as different as a square, & you can "try from every angle," but you cannot ever fix someone in life. Only they can fix themselves. You must be happy with yourself before you are happy with someone else. This is as transparent as your reflection on water with no wind because you can see yourself so clearly on the surface, but on the deep end, there are many dangers lying in the depths. Once you realize that the sky above is your limit & you can fly free like the birds above & the wind can be beneath your wings, then you WILL fly, & you will see that you are above the water. So, do not try. Just be free as a bird, & fly."

"Time is a tricky companion in life. There IS a difference in needing/wanting time. Choose to WANT time because it can leave you INCREDIBLY grateful in the end!!!"

December 13th

"Shoulda, woulda, & coulda NEVER 'could' DO 'ANY' thing!!!

December 14th

"Dancing is how you free the spirit."

"It is beautiful in life that no matter how 'far' you go in life, you NEVER STOP learning about yourself & the people around you."

December 16th

"In life, some have to work hard at life to get rich. Yet, you can be rich at heart & never have to work hard at life."

December 17th

"Life is a concert... ROCK IT!!"

"Word of the day: Superbilicious. Definition: blend of superb & delicious. Example as used in a sentence: HAVE A SUPERBILICIOUS DAY EVERYONE!!!

THE MUSIC

December 19th

"She comes into your life like a person in the crowd at a concert. It is like you are the one on stage performing. She has been waiting to see you this whole time, & you are there just to rock her world. If she were at the concert, she would rock his world just as equally. So, the man on stage just pours his heart & soul into his song & dance of life for her as they meet for the first time, never wanting the beat of their hearts or 'the music' of love at first sight… to stop."

December 20th

"Dreams are the circumference of the subconscious that you cause yourself to slip into."

December 21st

"If you were a concert... you would ROCK!!!"

December 22nd

"Life is about becoming the storm, dancing like lightning, burning the skies with your achievements, & striking destiny with passion & the glory of love."

December 23rd

"Life can never knock you down. Rather, its mistakes just make you stronger for victory."

December 24th

"A heart that touches, heals a broken one."

CHRISTMAS REFLECTION

Christmas Day Dec. 25th

"Things happen around holidays, deaths, tragedies, & circumstances of these kinds to bring families & friends closer together. It is not easy, but it is a spiritual sense of gathering. I know that may sound dark, but there is a light of love in it if you are able to see it. It sucks majorly but the spark of our loved one's spirits is to be continued into the Holiday season. Their memories, their laughs, their smiles, their joy is what is to be remembered most. Tis the season to be jolly they say... is it folly to be happy during this time of need when someone is so lonely? Remember the ones who have passed on because it is through their spirit that we must pass on their spirit to enlighten others & share what is so great about them, how much love they had, & how much love there really is to share about this season. Merry Christmas to all this season."

December 26th

"Live for life. Love to live. Live for love. Be a lover not a fighter, 'but'… FIGHT FOR LOVE!!!"

December 27th

"Life is a jigsaw puzzle…"

December 28th

"It is good to know what one disagrees on, that way two can agree within a medium."

383

December 29th

"Love is tricky... as is this entity we call life."

"People love a good game. Do not make bets, they do not always work out. Fifty percent of life is directed at you… fifty percent is not. Make peace, not war. Do not always follow the crowd because it is not always 'the right or correct way in your way.' Remember the good & forget the bad. Assume the best of people the best you can. Avoid being critical. Take life in moderation & take life with a pinch of salt. Do not fight the good fight, meaning do not fight the fight that does not need fighting. Fight your inner self. Fight life. Pick & choose your battles. Fight for freedom from your fears, tears, & the anxieties that shackle you with burden & stress that cause havoc in your everyday life. Grow so that you can flourish with prosperity. Do not ask rhetorical questions.

Greed is the worst, so forget it. Bullies are evil… never be one. We are all connected in this place, so connect. Stray from isolation, seek love at all costs as love is a treasured gift. It will strike evil in its ugly face against temptation by doing what is the 'right thing' consciously. Have fun, be silly, because viciousness is infectious, & if you can, live vicariously through someone or something. Travel. Love. Live. Laugh. Have fun. Be yourself. Do not let someone tell you who you are unless it is family, friends, or God. Fight for yourself, love all, & strive for perfection because this life is yours to succeed with. You are your best weapon of success. Now succeed & live. You have this, always."

"All we can do is who we are, & if it is something right…
then that is the best thing to look back on."

"Cheers & Journey Well."--J.M.P.